MODERN WORLD LEADERS

Ehud Olmert

MODERN WORLD LEADERS

Michelle Bachelet

Tony Blair

George W. Bush

Felipe Calderón

Hugo Chávez

Jacques Chirac

Hu Jintao

Hamid Karzai

Ali Khamenei

Kim Jong Il

Thabo Mbeki

Angela Merkel

Hosni Mubarak

Pervez Musharraf

Ehud Olmert

Pope Benedict XVI

Pope John Paul II

Roh Moo Hyun

Vladimir Putin

The Saudi Royal Family

Ariel Sharon

Viktor Yushchenko

Ehud Olmert

Dennis Abrams

CHELSEA HOUSE
PUBLISHERS
An imprint of Infobase Publishing

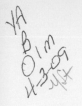

Ehud Olmert

Copyright © 2008 by Infobase Publishing

Chelsea House
An imprint of Infobase Publishing
132 West 31st Street
New York, NY 10001

Library of Congress Cataloging-in-Publication Data
Abrams, Dennis, 1960-
  Ehud Olmert / Dennis Abrams.
    p. cm. — (Modern world leaders)
  Includes bibliographical references and index.
  ISBN 978-0-7910-9761-8 (hardcover)
  1. Olmert, Ehud, 1945- 2. Prime ministers—Israel—Biography. 3. Israel—Politics and government. I. Title. II. Series.
  DS126.6.O44A27 2008
  956.9405'4092—dc22
  [B]   2008004876

Chelsea House books are available at special discounts when purchased in bulk quantities for businesses, associations, institutions, or sales promotions. Please call our Special Sales Department in New York at (212) 967-8800 or (800) 322-8755.

You can find Chelsea House on the World Wide Web at http://www.chelseahouse.com

Text design by Erik Lindstrom
Cover design by Takeshi Takahashi

Printed in the United States of America

Bang EJB 10 9 8 7 6 5 4 3 2 1

This book is printed on acid-free paper.

All links and Web addresses were checked and verified to be correct at the time of publication. Because of the dynamic nature of the Web, some addresses and links may have changed since publication and may no longer be valid.

TABLE OF CONTENTS

On Leadership

Leadership, it may be said, is really what makes the world go round. Love no doubt smoothes the passage; but love is a private transaction between consenting adults. Leadership is a public transaction with history. The idea of leadership affirms the capacity of individuals to move, inspire, and mobilize masses of people so that they act together in pursuit of an end. Sometimes leadership serves good purposes, sometimes bad; but whether the end is benign or evil, great leaders are those men and women who leave their personal stamp on history.

Now, the very concept of leadership implies the proposition that individuals can make a difference. This proposition has never been universally accepted. From classical times to the present day, eminent thinkers have regarded individuals as no more than the agents and pawns of larger forces, whether the gods and goddesses of the ancient world or, in the modern era, race, class, nation, the dialectic, the will of the people, the spirit of the times, history itself. Against such forces, the individual dwindles into insignificance.

So contends the thesis of historical determinism. Tolstoy's great novel *War and Peace* offers a famous statement of the case. Why, Tolstoy asked, did millions of men in the Napoleonic Wars, denying their human feelings and their common sense, move back and forth across Europe slaughtering their fellows? "The war," Tolstoy answered, "was bound to happen simply because it was bound to happen." All prior history determined it. As for leaders, they, Tolstoy said, "are but the labels that serve to give a name to an end and, like labels, they have the least possible

6

connection with the event." The greater the leader, "the more conspicuous the inevitability and the predestination of every act he commits." The leader, said Tolstoy, is "the slave of history."

Determinism takes many forms. Marxism is the determinism of class. Nazism the determinism of race. But the idea of men and women as the slaves of history runs athwart the deepest human instincts. Rigid determinism abolishes the idea of human freedom—the assumption of free choice that underlies every move we make, every word we speak, every thought we think. It abolishes the idea of human responsibility, since it is manifestly unfair to reward or punish people for actions that are by definition beyond their control. No one can live consistently by any deterministic creed. The Marxist states prove this themselves by their extreme susceptibility to the cult of leadership.

More than that, history refutes the idea that individuals make no difference. In December 1931, a British politician crossing Fifth Avenue in New York City between 76th and 77th streets around 10:30 P.M. looked in the wrong direction and was knocked down by an automobile—a moment, he later recalled, of a man aghast, a world aglare: "I do not understand why I was not broken like an eggshell or squashed like a gooseberry." Fourteen months later an American politician, sitting in an open car in Miami, Florida, was fired on by an assassin; the man beside him was hit. Those who believe that individuals make no difference to history might well ponder whether the next two decades would have been the same had Mario Constasino's car killed Winston Churchill in 1931 and Giuseppe Zangara's bullet killed Franklin Roosevelt in 1933. Suppose, in addition, that Lenin had died of typhus in Siberia in 1895 and that Hitler had been killed on the western front in 1916. What would the twentieth century have looked like now?

For better or for worse, individuals do make a difference. "The notion that a people can run itself and its affairs anonymously," wrote the philosopher William James, "is now well known to be the silliest of absurdities. Mankind does nothing save through initiatives on the part of inventors, great or small, and imitation by the rest of us—these are the sole factors in human progress. Individuals of genius show the way, and set the patterns, which common people then adopt and follow."

Leadership, James suggests, means leadership in thought as well as in action. In the long run, leaders in thought may well make the greater difference to the world. "The ideas of economists and political philosophers, both when they are right and when they are wrong," wrote John Maynard Keynes, "are more powerful than is commonly understood. Indeed the world is ruled by little else. Practical men, who believe themselves to be quite exempt from any intellectual influences, are usually the slaves of some defunct economist. . . . The power of vested interests is vastly exaggerated compared with the gradual encroachment of ideas."

But, as Woodrow Wilson once said, "Those only are leaders of men, in the general eye, who lead in action. . . . It is at their hands that new thought gets its translation into the crude language of deeds." Leaders in thought often invent in solitude and obscurity, leaving to later generations the tasks of imitation. Leaders in action—the leaders portrayed in this series—have to be effective in their own time.

And they cannot be effective by themselves. They must act in response to the rhythms of their age. Their genius must be adapted, in a phrase from William James, "to the receptivities of the moment." Leaders are useless without followers. "There goes the mob," said the French politician, hearing a clamor in the streets. "I am their leader. I must follow them." Great leaders turn the inchoate emotions of the mob to purposes of their own. They seize on the opportunities of their time, the hopes, fears, frustrations, crises, potentialities. They succeed when events have prepared the way for them, when the community is awaiting to be aroused, when they can provide the clarifying and organizing ideas. Leadership completes the circuit between the individual and the mass and thereby alters history.

It may alter history for better or for worse. Leaders have been responsible for the most extravagant follies and most monstrous crimes that have beset suffering humanity. They have also been vital in such gains as humanity has made in individual freedom, religious and racial tolerance, social justice, and respect for human rights.

There is no sure way to tell in advance who is going to lead for good and who for evil. But a glance at the gallery of men and women in MODERN WORLD LEADERS suggests some useful tests.

One test is this: Do leaders lead by force or by persuasion? By command or by consent? Through most of history leadership was exercised by the divine right of authority. The duty of followers was to defer and to obey. "Theirs not to reason why/Theirs but to do and die." On occasion, as with the so-called enlightened despots of the eighteenth century in Europe, absolutist leadership was animated by humane purposes. More often, absolutism nourished the passion for domination, land, gold, and conquest and resulted in tyranny.

The great revolution of modern times has been the revolution of equality. "Perhaps no form of government," wrote the British historian James Bryce in his study of the United States, *The American Commonwealth*, "needs great leaders so much as democracy." The idea that all people should be equal in their legal condition has undermined the old structure of authority, hierarchy, and deference. The revolution of equality has had two contrary effects on the nature of leadership. For equality, as Alexis de Tocqueville pointed out in his great study *Democracy in America*, might mean equality in servitude as well as equality in freedom.

"I know of only two methods of establishing equality in the political world," Tocqueville wrote. "Rights must be given to every citizen, or none at all to anyone . . . save one, who is the master of all." There was no middle ground "between the sovereignty of all and the absolute power of one man." In his astonishing prediction of twentieth-century totalitarian dictatorship, Tocqueville explained how the revolution of equality could lead to the *Führerprinzip* and more terrible absolutism than the world had ever known.

But when rights are given to every citizen and the sovereignty of all is established, the problem of leadership takes a new form, becomes more exacting than ever before. It is easy to issue commands and enforce them by the rope and the stake, the concentration camp and the *gulag*. It is much harder to use argument and achievement to overcome opposition and win consent. The Founding Fathers of the United States understood the difficulty. They believed that history had given them the opportunity to decide, as Alexander Hamilton wrote in the first Federalist Paper, whether men are indeed capable of basing government on "reflection and choice, or whether they are forever destined to depend . . . on accident and force."

Government by reflection and choice called for a new style of leadership and a new quality of followership. It required leaders to be responsive to popular concerns, and it required followers to be active and informed participants in the process. Democracy does not eliminate emotion from politics; sometimes it fosters demagoguery; but it is confident that, as the greatest of democratic leaders put it, you cannot fool all of the people all of the time. It measures leadership by results and retires those who overreach or falter or fail.

It is true that in the long run despots are measured by results too. But they can postpone the day of judgment, sometimes indefinitely, and in the meantime they can do infinite harm. It is also true that democracy is no guarantee of virtue and intelligence in government, for the voice of the people is not necessarily the voice of God. But democracy, by assuring the right of opposition, offers built-in resistance to the evils inherent in absolutism. As the theologian Reinhold Niebuhr summed it up, "Man's capacity for justice makes democracy possible, but man's inclination to justice makes democracy necessary."

A second test for leadership is the end for which power is sought. When leaders have as their goal the supremacy of a master race or the promotion of totalitarian revolution or the acquisition and exploitation of colonies or the protection of greed and privilege or the preservation of personal power, it is likely that their leadership will do little to advance the cause of humanity. When their goal is the abolition of slavery, the liberation of women, the enlargement of opportunity for the poor and powerless, the extension of equal rights to racial minorities, the defense of the freedoms of expression and opposition, it is likely that their leadership will increase the sum of human liberty and welfare.

Leaders have done great harm to the world. They have also conferred great benefits. You will find both sorts in this series. Even "good" leaders must be regarded with a certain wariness. Leaders are not demigods; they put on their trousers one leg after another just like ordinary mortals. No leader is infallible, and every leader needs to be reminded of this at regular intervals. Irreverence irritates leaders but is their salvation. Unquestioning submission corrupts leaders and demeans followers. Making a cult of a leader is always a mistake. Fortunately hero worship generates its own antidote. "Every hero," said Emerson, "becomes a bore at last."

The single benefit the great leaders confer is to embolden the rest of us to live according to our own best selves, to be active, insistent, and resolute in affirming our own sense of things. For great leaders attest to the reality of human freedom against the supposed inevitabilities of history. And they attest to the wisdom and power that may lie within the most unlikely of us, which is why Abraham Lincoln remains the supreme example of great leadership. A great leader, said Emerson, exhibits new possibilities to all humanity. "We feed on genius. . . . Great men exist that there may be greater men."

Great leaders, in short, justify themselves by emancipating and empowering their followers. So humanity struggles to master its destiny, remembering with Alexis de Tocqueville: "It is true that around every man a fatal circle is traced beyond which he cannot pass; but within the wide verge of that circle he is powerful and free; as it is with man, so with communities." ●

1

"Severe Failure"

IN LEBANON IT'S KNOWN AS THE JULY WAR. ISRAEL KNOWS IT AS THE Second Lebanon War. And to the rest of the world it's known as the 2006 Lebanon War. The opponents were Hezbollah (literally "party of God"), a Shia Islamic political and paramilitary (some would call it terrorist) organization based in Lebanon and led by Sayyed Hassan Nasrallah, and the nation of Israel, led by Prime Minister Ehud Olmert. The battle itself took place in Lebanon and northern Israel.

The conflict began on July 12, 2006, when a Hezbollah ground contingent crossed the Lebanese border into Israeli territory. There, they attacked two Israeli armored Humvees patrolling on the Israeli side of the Israel–Lebanon border near Zar'it, killing three, injuring two, and abducting two Israeli soldiers. This incident triggered a war that continued unabated until a United Nations–brokered cease-fire went into effect on August 14, 2006, and Israel lifted its naval blockade of Lebanon on September 8, 2006.

The month-long conflict killed more than 1,000 people, most of them Lebanese. The Lebanese infrastructure (roads, bridges, etc.) was severely damaged. Also, 974,184 Lebanese were displaced and driven from their homes. Between 300,000 and 500,000 Israelis were displaced as well.

Even today, more than two years since the cease-fire went into effect, much of southern Lebanon remains uninhabitable due to unexploded cluster bombs. At the end of 2006, an estimated 200,000 Lebanese still remained displaced or living as refugees.

When the war finally concluded, no one was quite certain who had won. The nations of Iran and Syria proclaimed victory for their Hezbollah allies. Israel and the United States publicly declared that Hezbollah had lost the conflict. But among the Israelis themselves, a consensus soon built that they had, indeed, lost the war. And by August 25, 2006, just two weeks after declaring "victory," 63 percent of Israelis wanted Israeli prime minister Ehud Olmert to resign from office.

In an article entitled "Hizbullah's Shallow Victory," the magazine *Economist* summed up many of the reasons why so many Israelis considered the war to be a defeat. It wasn't so much that they felt that Israel had actually *lost* the war. But because they had not actually defeated Hezbollah, Israelis believed they had handed Hezbollah a symbolic victory in the eyes of the Arab world.

This was due to the fact that Hezbollah had been able to defend itself on Lebanese soil while still being able to inflict damaging and highly demoralizing rocket attacks aimed largely at Israeli civilians. And, it was able to do this in the face of a punishing air and land campaign by the Israel Defense Forces (IDF), whose numbers and military might far exceeded that of Hezbollah. The *Economist* concluded that by simply surviving this unequal David vs. Goliath battle, Hezbollah had emerged with both a military and political victory.

Not only that, but going into the war, Israel's goals were to rescue its two abducted soldiers and destroy the military

Israeli reserve soldiers and activists gather at the grave of former prime minister Golda Meir in 2006 to protest Israeli leadership *(above)*. The Israel-Lebanon conflict in 2006 was wildly unpopular with the Israeli public, and many protested and called for Olmert to resign from his post. While both sides claimed victory in the battle, many Israelis believed their country lost the war.

capability of Hezbollah. Neither of those goals were achieved. Indeed, far from being destroyed, Hezbollah is rapidly rearming and leading the rebuilding effort in southern Lebanon. This rebuilding, done with support from Iran, has given Hezbollah even greater political clout.

In the aftermath of what the Israeli public saw as a disastrous war, the Israeli government launched a commission. Its assignment was to investigate the events leading up to the war and then to examine how the war itself was conducted. The commission, led by retired judge Eliyahu Winograd, issued a partial report on April 30, 2007. It is known as the Winograd Report.

THE WINOGRAD REPORT

The report, remarkably honest and open for any government-appointed commission, did not hesitate to lay blame or to name names. It stated that the Israeli defense minister, Amir Peretz, had been unaware of the state and lack of preparedness of the IDF, even though he should have been fully aware. He "did not have knowledge or experience in military, political or governmental matters. He also did not have good knowledge of the basic principles of using military force to achieve political goals," the report stated.

Despite these deficiencies, the report went on to say, "he made his decisions during this period without systemic consultations with experienced political and professional experts, including outside the security establishment." In fact the panel found that "his serving as minister of defense during the war impaired Israel's ability to respond well to its challenges."

The Israeli chief of staff of the IDF, Dan Halutz, was criticized as well for entering the war "unprepared" and for failing to inform the cabinet of the true state of the IDF before the war began. According to the findings, the army and its chief of staff "were not prepared for the event of the abduction despite recurring alerts."

The commission aimed its harshest criticism squarely at Prime Minister Olmert. It said that Olmert "bears supreme and comprehensive responsibility for the decisions of 'his' government and the operations of the army."

The report also said that "the prime minister made up his mind hastily, despite the fact that no detailed military plan was submitted to him and without asking for one. He made his decision without . . . consultation with others . . . despite not having experience in external-political and military affairs."

Olmert was also criticized for lack of flexibility and for failing to change his plans once it became clear that the war was not progressing as expected. "All of these," the report said, "add up to a serious failure in exercising judgment, responsibility and prudence."

The report was a devastating attack on Olmert's ability to lead and on his standing as prime minister. Despite this, Olmert vowed to stay on as prime minister, resisting calls for his immediate resignation.

Ironically, the report was issued just a little more than a year after Olmert's political party, Kadima, had won the 2006 national elections, thereby setting the stage for him to become only the twelfth person to serve as Israel's prime minister. On the other hand, it was only because of the fact that the previous prime minister, Ariel Sharon, had become incapacitated by a stroke that his top aide Olmert became acting prime minister, and finally, was elected prime minister in his own right.

This happened despite the fact, as the *New York Times* pointed out, that Olmert had never been very popular with the Israeli public. Best known as a "wheeler-dealer" and a cigar-smoking lawyer rather than for his charisma or courage on the battlefield, he was definitely not the type of person typically selected to be prime minister of Israel.

In fact, in a poll published shortly before the election, Israeli voters were asked what they liked about Ehud Olmert. More than 30 percent liked nothing. Nearly 29 percent valued his courage to state his position, and 19 percent liked his "wisdom and cleverness." Fewer than 15 percent valued his experience. These are not exactly the kind of numbers that indicate a greatly loved candidate.

After serving as minister of various government departments, Ehud Olmert gained popularity during his terms as mayor of Jerusalem. Olmert's success as mayor earned him the opportunity to work closely with Prime Minister Ariel Sharon *(above left, with Olmert)*, who made Olmert the deputy prime minister of Israel.

But as Ari Shavit, a writer for the Israeli newspaper *Haaretz* pointed out, "Ehud Olmert is a very skilled politician, intelligent and cool-headed." Through a steady progression of jobs, from member of the Knesset (the Israeli legislature) at the age of twenty-eight to mayor of Jerusalem to Ariel Sharon's right-hand man, Olmert kept his eye on the main chance, wait-ing for his opportunity to fulfill his life's dream—to become prime minister of Israel.

As prime minister, he was in a position to help bring about a lasting peace for Israel. He had primarily been known as a defiantly right-wing politician, one who had voted against every peace treaty that Israel ever signed. But in recent years, he had grown to embrace the idea that in order to make peace, Israel would have to give up territory won in the Six Days' War of 1967. If Olmert could manage to bring about a peaceful solution to the Palestinian problem, one that had eluded previ-ous prime ministers, his place in history would be secure.

But, just one year after his election, his chances of even remaining prime minister seemed iffy at best. With his popu-larity dropping daily (one television station poll had his favor-ability rating at just 3 percent!), it remained an open question as to just how long he would be able to hold on to power.

What went wrong? How did a man who spent his life wanting to become prime minister go so disastrously wrong in just his first year of office? How did he achieve his dream, and would he be able to continue to serve as prime minister? How did Ehud Olmert get to where he was?

2

Zionism

TO GET A TRUE SENSE OF WHO EHUD OLMERT IS, AND TO UNDERSTAND THE root causes of the 2006 Lebanon War, it is necessary to go back approximately 2,000 years. Without looking at the events that led to the creation of the modern state of Israel and the anger and turmoil that its creation caused throughout the Middle East, there's little chance of even beginning to understand the events of today. It would be like walking into a movie halfway through the screening—you'd have no real grasp of the plot, or the characters, or what it is that drives and motivates the characters. It's the same with the Middle East and Ehud Olmert.

THE HOLY LAND

While it's true that Jews, Christians, and Muslims all claim the land that is now the modern state of Israel as their own religion's Holy Land, it is also true that the Jews seem to have staked the earliest claim. Jewish tradition holds that the land of Israel has been the Holy Land and Promised Land for nearly 4,000 years, since the time of the biblical patriarchs, Abraham, Isaac, and Jacob. The land of Israel contains Judaism's most important religious sites, including the First and Second Temples of Jerusalem.

Politically speaking, it was sometime around the eleventh century B.C. that the first of a series of Jewish kingdoms and states established rule over the region. These Jewish kingdoms and states would maintain fairly continuous rule over the region for the next 1,000 years.

Later, under the successive rule of Assyrians, Babylonians, Persians, Greeks, Romans, and Byzantines, the Jewish presence in the region shrank, largely due to multiple forced expulsions. One of the most famous of these forced expulsions occurred after the failure of Bar Kokhba's revolt against the Roman Empire.

BAR KOKHBA REVOLT

After the failure of the Great Jewish Revolt in the year A.D. 70, the Roman authorities took extra care to suppress the still rebellious province. Initially, the Roman emperor Hadrian appeared to be sympathetic toward his Jewish subjects. But when it was learned that he planned to rebuild the Jew's holy city of Jerusalem as a pagan metropolis, with a new temple dedicated to Jupiter to be built over the ruins of the Second Temple, it was too much for the Jews to accept.

The year 132 saw the beginning of an armed revolt led by Simon Bar Kokhba. It lasted for three years, before finally being crushed in the summer of 135. After losing Jerusalem, Bar Kokhba and the remains of his army withdrew to the fortress of Betar, where they came under siege. According to the Jerusalem Talmud, the numbers slain were so enormous that the Romans "went on killing until their horses were submerged in blood to their nostrils."

According to the Roman historian Cassius Dio, 580,000 Jews were killed, and 50 fortified towns and 985 villages were razed to the ground. Hadrian attempted to root out Judaism from the region, since he saw it as the cause of continuous rebellions. He prohibited Torah law and the Jewish calendar, and executed Judaic scholars. At the former temple sanctuary, he installed two statues, one of the Roman god Jupiter and another of himself.

And, in an attempt to erase any memory of the state of Judea, he simply took the name off the map and replaced it with "Syria Palaestina." The "new" state was named after the Philistines, the ancient biblical enemy of the Jews. Since then, the land has been referred to as "Palestine," which took the place of earlier names "Iudaea" (Judaea) and the ancient "Canaan."

In the same vein, Hadrian reestablished Jerusalem as the Roman pagan polis (city) of Aelia Capitolina, and Jews were forbidden from entering it.

AFTERMATH AND DIASPORA

Many modern historians have come to regard the Bar Kokhba Revolt as the beginning of the Jewish Diaspora—the dispersal of Jews from their traditional homeland. But despite living in exile from their homeland, dispersed throughout the Middle East, Europe, Asia, and eventually North and South America, the Jewish people longed to return to the Promised Land. As is said hopefully at the end of every Passover seder ceremony, "Next year in Jerusalem!"

This is not to say, of course, that the land that would become Israel was without Jews during the long years of the Diaspora. Although Jews were not allowed into Jerusalem by the Romans (with the exception of a once-a-year ceremony of mourning at the Western Wall of the temple), the main Jewish population simply moved from the city to Galilee. It was there that the Jerusalem Talmud, one of Judaism's

PUB. ÆL. ADRIAN.

Almost 2,000 years ago, the Roman emperor Hadrian *(above)* attempted to rebuild the Jewish holy site of Jerusalem as a Roman city and triggered a Jewish rebellion. Despite his reputation for being a progressive and generous ruler, Hadrian brutally quashed the uprising and renamed the entire Jewish kingdom Syria Palaestina, which later became known as Palestine.

NO MATTER WHERE THEY LIVED, THE JEWISH PEOPLE CONTINUED TO SEE THE LAND OF ISRAEL AS THEIR SPIRITUAL HOME.

most important texts, was composed in the years after the expulsion.

With the collapse of the Roman Empire, control of Palestine shifted to the Byzantine Empire. Palestine fell to the initial Muslim conquests around A.D. 636. Control of the region then transferred between the Umayyads, the Abbasids, the European Crusaders, the Khwarezmians, and the Mongols over the next six centuries, before falling into the hands of the Mamluk Sultinate in 1260. In 1517, the land of Israel became part of the Ottoman (Turkish) Empire, which would rule the region until the twentieth century.

LONGING TO RETURN

No matter where they lived, the Jewish people continued to see the land of Israel as their spiritual home. For generations, the universal belief was that the Jewish people would return to Israel with the coming of the Messiah. In other words, only after divine intervention would a new Jewish state be possible. Throughout the centuries, some Jewish leaders proposed or attempted a return without waiting for the Messiah, but they were in a distinct minority.

Between the thirteenth and nineteenth centuries, though, the number of those who made what was known as the *aliyah* (literally "ascent"; Jewish immigration to the land of Israel) rose. Jews from Spain, France, Italy, the Germanic states, Russia, and North Africa began immigrating in small numbers to Palestine, in large part fleeing religious persecution.

Who was occupying the Jews' ancestral land when these immigrants arrived? By the mid-nineteenth century, Palestine was a part of the Ottoman Empire, populated mostly by Muslim and Christian Arabs, as well as lesser numbers of Jews, Greeks, Druze, Bedouins, and other minorities. This population, which had inhabited the land for generations, understandably did not recognize the Jews' historic claims to the land. They saw the land as theirs and felt no need to give anything back to the previous occupants.

By 1844, because of a slow, steady stream of immigrants, Jews made up the largest population group (and by 1890 an absolute majority) in a few cities, primarily Jerusalem (although as a whole, the Jewish population in Palestine still made up less than 10 percent of the total). Those numbers, however, would soon change.

In 1862, the Jewish philosopher Moses Hess published *Rome and Jerusalem*, a book that advocated the establishment of a socialist Jewish state in the land of Israel. Many heeded the call, and in 1881, the first large wave of modern immigration to Israel began, as Jews fled growing persecution in eastern Europe.

But despite the impact of Hess, Theodor Herzl (1860–1904), an Austro-Hungarian Jew, is usually credited with founding the modern Zionist movement. The publication of his book *Der Judenstaat* (*The Jewish State*), in which he called for the establishment of a Jewish state, is regarded as a milestone in the history of Zionism.

In 1897, the First Zionist Congress proclaimed the decision "to establish a home for the Jewish people in Eretz Yisrael [Hebrew for "Land of Israel"] secured under public law." This proclamation, which led to an influx of approximately 40,000 additional Jews into Palestine between the years 1904 and 1914, was bolstered in 1917 by the British government.

In that year, British foreign secretary Arthur Balfour issued the Balfour Declaration, which "view[ed] with favour the establishment in Palestine of a national home for the Jewish people . . . it being clearly understood that nothing shall be done which may prejudice the civil and religious rights of existing non-Jewish communities in Palestine."

This declaration was supported by a number of other countries, including the United States. It became even more important in the years following World War I (1914–1918). Then, with the end of the Ottoman Empire, the League of Nations assigned control of Palestine to the United Kingdom with the Palestine Mandate.

Jewish immigration grew slowly throughout the 1920s, when more than 100,000 Jews returned to the region. It increased substantially during the 1930s, due to political turmoil in Europe and Nazi persecution. Nearly 250,000 additional Jews immigrated to Palestine during this period, until immigration restrictions (the MacDonald White Paper) were imposed by the United Kingdom in 1939, perhaps in response to the 1936–1939 Arab revolt in Palestine.

Regardless, due to the Holocaust, Adolf Hitler's attempt to exterminate the Jews of Europe, many Jews fled illegally to Israel, their one "safe haven." By the end of World War II, despite British bans on Jewish immigration, Jews accounted for 33 percent of the population of Palestine, up from just 11 percent in 1922.

In the meantime, many Arabs, opposed to the Balfour Declaration, the Palestine Mandate, and the very idea of a Jewish national home, had instigated riots and pogroms against Jews in the region. As a result of a series of attacks in 1921, the Haganah was formed to protect Jewish settlements.

The Haganah was largely defensive in nature, leading several members to split off and form the Irgun in 1931. The Irgun took a much more offensive approach to the ongoing situation, including deadly attacks against the British, in an effort to force them to leave Palestine. The British would soon have plenty of reasons to end the Palestine Mandate.

THE HOLOCAUST AND THE BIRTH OF ISRAEL

When World War II ended in 1945, the conscience of the world was shocked and aroused as the full scope of the Holocaust became apparent. With 6 million Jews murdered at the hands of the Nazis, the need for a Jewish homeland became even more urgent. The guilt of the nations that allowed the Holocaust to happen, together with the pleas from the survivors for a safe land of their own, combined to make a Jewish homeland both a political and moral necessity.

Events began moving rapidly in 1947. The British, facing increasing levels of Arab-Jewish violence in Palestine as well as the world's desire to create a Jewish state and a homeland for the survivors of the concentration camps, decided to withdraw from the Mandate of Palestine. That same year the newly created United Nations approved the 1947 UN Partition Plan.

This plan would split Palestine into three parts: a Jewish state with a majority Jewish population; an Arab state with a majority Arab population; and an International Zone to be administered by the United Nations, comprising Jerusalem and the surrounding area where the Jewish and Arab populations would be roughly equal.

By a vote of 33 to 13, the United Nations approved the plan on November 28, 1947. It was felt that this was the best possible solution, allowing both the Jews and the Palestinians a homeland of their own.

David Ben-Gurion, architect of the Haganah and later the first prime minister of Israel, tentatively accepted the UN Partition Plan. The Arab League, as well as most of the Arabs of Palestine, rejected it. They felt it unfair that the Zionists should receive so much of Palestine when they owned only about 6 percent of the land and made up only one-third of the population.

The Arab Higher Committee immediately ordered a violent three-day strike on Jewish civilians, buildings, shops and

אם כל משה ועדיין אנו לא אל המנ

Hitler's attempt to exterminate Europe's Jewish population caused a mass exodus of Jews from the continent. Many of these refugees jumped aboard ships that took them to Palestine. *Above*, a boat carrying 450 Jewish survivors reaches Haifa, a city on the Mediterranean Sea. Their banner reads "Keep the gates open, we are not the last."

neighborhoods. This, along with an insurgency organized by underground Jewish militias, soon turned into widespread fighting between Arabs and Jews and the beginnings of the 1948 Arab-Israeli War.

Despite the state of near turmoil, Israel was officially proclaimed an independent nation on May 14, 1948, just one day before the expiration of the British Mandate of Palestine. Following the formal establishment of the State of Israel, the armies of five Arab countries declared war on Israel, beginning the second stage of the 1948 Arab-Israeli War.

To many, it seemed likely that the Jewish state would be destroyed before it even began, and with it, the hopes and dreams of Mordechai and Belle Olmert, who had made their own return to Palestine in 1933.

3

Roots

LIKE MANY MEMBERS OF THE DIASPORA, THE OLMERT FAMILY FOUND THE
road back to Palestine long and difficult. The very origin of the
name "Olmert" is not known, even to members of the family.
It is known that Ehud's great-great-grandfather had been
kidnapped as a young child by the army of the Russian tsar and
forced to serve in it for twenty-five years. When he was finally
released, he settled in the city of Samara along the River Volga.
And when he was asked for his name, he gave it as Olmert;
the family speculates that he remembered it in a distorted way
from his childhood.

Ehud's father, Mordechai, was born in 1911. The family did
well and even prospered in Samara. But the days when Jews
could live in relative peace in Russia were rapidly coming to an
end. With the Russian (Bolshevik) Revolution of 1917, Russia's
historic anti-Semitism (a prejudice, dislike, or hatred of Jews)

came forward, and the Jews of Samara, as in so many other Russian towns and cities, became the scapegoats.

The Olmert family fled Russia to Manchuria in northeastern China, where they had business connections. The Olmerts settled in the town of Tzitzikar near Harbin. Young Mordechai hoped that the family could soon move to Harbin itself, a large city that, somewhat surprisingly, was home to a sizable number of Jews.

Indeed, as Li Shuxiao, the director of the Jewish Research Center of the Heilonjiang Provincial Academy of Social Sciences pointed out in the newspaper *China Daily*, "Historically, Harbin was once the largest political, economic, and cultural centre for the Jews in the Far East Region. At the end of the 19th century, a lot of European Jews migrated to Harbin with the construction of the Mid-East railway. In the 1920s, the number of Jews in Harbin reached its peak of more than 20,000." It was there in Harbin that Mordechai hoped that he would be able to pursue his growing interest in Jewish affairs.

Mordechai got his wish when he was 16, when the family settled in Harbin. He became involved in Zionist activity, but he was not satisfied with the only movement that existed in Harbin at that time, HaShomer HaTzair. HaShomer HaTzair, which translates as "the Youth Guard," was a Socialist-Zionist youth movement founded in 1913. It believed that the liberation of Jewish youth could be accomplished by aliyah to Palestine and living in kibbutzim, communal or collective farms.

Instead, inspired by the personality of a man named Ze'ev Jabotinsky, Mordechai Olmert became drawn to the Revisionist Movement, beginning a lifelong dedication to the cause. Unlike the "practical Zionism" of David Ben-Gurion and Chaim Weizmann, which was focused on independent settlement of Eretz Yisrael, Revisionist Zionism was based on a vision of "political Zionism." This included initial cooperation with Britain on transforming the entire Mandate of Palestine into a sovereign Jewish state, without a separate state for the Palestinian people.

Recruiting a group of other young people, Mordechai established a local chapter of the Betar Youth Movement, the Revisionist Zionist youth movement in Harbin. (Betar itself was named after the ancient Judean city of Betar, where Simon Bar Kokhba had made his valiant last stand against the Romans in A.D. 135.) It was there that Mordechai met the women who would become his wife, Bella Vugman, herself a dedicated member of the Betar Movement.

Under Mordechai's leadership, Betar became the dominant Zionist movement in Harbin, drawing in Jewish members of many other movements. Interestingly, unlike most of the other Jewish émigrés living in Harbin, Mordechai insisted on studying at a Chinese, rather than at a Russian, high school, and throughout his long life, he never forgot the Chinese language.

In 1930, deciding that the time for action had come, Mordechai and Bella left Harbin, beginning their journey to Palestine. After first stopping in Holland to study agriculture at a Hachshara (preparation or training) farm, he and Bella arrived in Palestine in 1933. They were finally home.

RESISTANCE

Arriving "home" didn't mean that the Olmerts could rest. The year 1933 saw the birth of the Irgun, and Mordechai and Bella immediately became involved. Indeed, they were among the group's founding members.

As previously mentioned, the Irgun (shorthand for Ha'Irgu Ha'Tsvai Ha'Leumi B'Eretz Yisrael, or National Military Organization in the Land of Israel) was a clandestine military Zionist group that operated in Palestine from 1931 to 1948. In Israel, the group is commonly referred to as "Etzel."

If the Haganah was created to defend Jewish settlers from Arab attack, Etzel made retaliation against Arab attacks a central part of its earliest efforts. The group was, in essence,

Ehud Olmert's parents were founding members of the Irgun, a Jewish military group that was dedicated to taking revenge against those who attacked Jews in Palestine. Their efforts to force out the British and fight for the formation of Israel proved somewhat successful. Above, the group marches through the city of Tel Aviv the night before the declaration of the Jewish homeland.

the armed expression of Revisionist Zionism, the movement that Mordechai Olmert had been a part of since he was a teenager.

The group's founder, Ze'ev Jabotinsky, famously stated that "every Jew had the right to enter Palestine; only active retaliation would deter the Arabs and the British; only Jewish armed force would ensure the Jewish state." As a movement, the Irgun was a direct predecessor to Israel's right-wing Herut, or "Freedom," Party, which led to today's Likud Party.

For the next fourteen years, both Mordechai and Bella Olmert actively participated in missions for the Irgun. At first, the group limited its activities to avenging attacks on Jewish settlers. For example, on August 17, 1936, after an Arab shooting at Carmel school in Tel Aviv, resulting in the death of a Jewish child, unnamed Irgun members attacked an Arab neighborhood near Kerem Hatemanim in Tel Aviv, killing one Arab man and injuring another.

On another occasion, on March 6, 1937, a Jew praying at the Western Wall in Jerusalem was shot by a local Arab. A few hours later, the Irgun shot an Arab in the Jerusalem neighborhood of Rechavia. It was this tit-for-tat, eye-for-an-eye action that continued until 1939.

With the issuing of the MacDonald White Paper, severely limiting the amount of Jewish immigration into Palestine, the Irgun began taking action against the British as well. They began sabotaging British facilities such as electric plants and radio and telephone lines.

With the end of World War II, the Irgun continued to fight on two fronts: protecting Jewish settlers from Arab attacks and putting pressure on the British to leave Palestine. It was into this land of turmoil, of constant attack and counterattack that Ehud Olmert was born on September 30, 1945, in the city of Binyamina, which was still part of the British Mandate of Palestine. (The city of Binyamina, which was located south of Haifa, no longer exists. In 2003 it merged with nearby Giv'at Ada into a local council now called Binyamina-Giv'at Ada.)

ISRAEL ACHIEVES INDEPENDENCE

By 1947, under continued pressure by the Irgun within Palestine, and from an outside world traumatized by the Holocaust, the British decided to withdraw from Palestine. With the United Nations vote to partition the land, it looked as though an independent land of Israel would soon be a reality.

With this, the Irgun began to prepare for Israel's defense. The chief commander of Etzel, Menachem Begin, made plans to ship weapons and fighters into the state. These plans included a ship to be named *Altalena*. To help raise funds for the ship and weapons, Begin turned to Mordechai Olmert.

Olmert returned to China, visiting Jewish communities throughout the country, working his way back to the city of his youth, Harbin. It is said that his charismatic appearance (along, no doubt, with his ability to speak Chinese) helped to raise the needed funds. Reportedly the Jewish women threw their jewelry on the table for him—anything to help their fellow Jews build a new homeland. With these efforts, Mordechai Olmert felt that he had come full circle in his life. He was able to use his past to help create a Jewish homeland for the many generations to come.

Although the Jews of Palestine were happy to be part of the new Jewish state, they knew that their struggle had just begun. The Arab Palestinians, along with their Arab allies, were not going to allow Palestine to be partitioned without a fight.

THE 1948 ARAB-ISRAELI WAR

On May 14, 1948, the State of Israel declared itself an independent nation, stating that "the land of Israel was the birthplace of the Jewish people. Here their spiritual, religious and political identity was shaped. Here they first attained to statehood, created cultural value of national and universal significance and gave to the world the eternal Book of Books (the Old Testament.)"

It goes on to discuss the years of exile, the Diaspora, and the horrors of the Holocaust before describing "the natural right of the Jewish people to be masters of their own fate, like all other nations, in their own sovereign State. Thus members and representatives of the Jews of Palestine and the Zionist movement upon the end of the British Mandate, by virtue of 'natural and historic right' and based on the United Nations resolution . . . Hereby declare the establishment of a Jewish state in the land of Israel to be known as the State of Israel." After nearly 2,000 years of exile, the Jews once again had a country to call their own.

By the end of May, approximately 6,000 Syrian, 4,500 Iraqi, between 6,000 and 9,000 Transjordanian, 1,000 Lebanese, and 5,500 Egyptian troops had invaded the newly formed state, joining the Arab Palestinians who had taken up arms against the Jews. But by the end of the war, against all odds, Israel had repulsed the invaders and held on to control all of the land that had been allotted to it. In addition, Israeli forces had captured nearly half of the territory that had been designated for the Arab state, as well as part of Jerusalem.

The war and the armistice agreements between Israel and its neighbors resulted in the division of the former British mandate into the State of Israel; the Gaza Strip, which was controlled by Egypt; and the West Bank, which was held by Transjordan.

For Israelis, the war and their remarkable victory over superior forces marked the successful establishment of the Israeli state. But for Palestinian Arabs, it signified the beginning of the events referred to as *al Nakba*, or "the Catastrophe." This term is used to describe the fleeing or forced expulsion of hundreds of thousands of Palestinian residents (UN estimates placed the number at 711,000) from the newly created State of Israel, as well as the subsequent Israeli ban (ostensibly

After the demarcation lines were drawn and Israel was declared a Jewish state, Palestinian Arabs were joined by almost 32,000 other Arabs from neighboring countries in an attempt to reclaim territory. They were defeated by Israeli forces, which successfully defended and expanded Israel's borders. *Above*, in a 1948 photograph, an Israeli armed guard rides a bus with blindfolded Arab prisoners on their way to questioning.

on security grounds) on their return. Many people might comment on the irony of a people who had once been expulsed from their homeland now forcing the expulsion of others.

To this day, historians argue over the true cause of al Nakba. Mainstream Israeli historians and the government of Israel claim that the main responsibility of the exodus falls on local and foreign Arab leaders who urged the Arab Palestinians to flee. Some Israeli historians and most Arab historians place the blame on Israel, saying that Israeli forces drove the Palestinians from their land. There is evidence to back up both points of view, so it is not unlikely that both explanations are at least partially true.

Whatever the cause, the problem of Palestinian refugees today remains unresolved and a constant source of political and military tension throughout the Middle East, one that Ehud Olmert was still trying to solve sixty years later. But this would be years in the future. On July 20, 1949, the final armistice agreement was signed (with Syria) and, at least for the moment, Israel was at peace. Ehud Olmert was just four years old. His parents had devoted their lives to the establishment of a Jewish homeland. Now that it was a reality, the hard work was just beginning.

4

Growing Pains

FOR THE FIRST THREE YEARS OF EHUD OLMERT'S LIFE, THE FAMILY LIVED in an old fortress that had been built by the Turks near the Mediterranean coast, just south of Haifa. Disguised as an agricultural settlement, the site was used by the Irgun to train its fighters before sending them out on missions. With independence and the establishment of the Jewish state, the Olmert family left the fortress. They settled in Binyamina, along with other members of the Herut movement, led by Menachem Begin. There, Mordechai and Bella, along with three-year-old Ehud, hoped to continue to play a prominent role in Israel's development.

Although Mordechai and Bella Olmert had devoted their lives to the cause of Israel, the next few years found them in political exile. The Irgun had long been labeled a terrorist organization by the British government. And now, despite the vital role it had taken in establishing Israel's independence, it had become an embarrassment to Israel's first prime minister, David Ben-Gurion, and the ruling Mapai Party, the predecessor of today's Labor Party.

After the Irgun was blamed for murdering a prominent member of the emerging labor movement, the organization was disbanded and condemned. After that, members associated with Irgun and the political party of the Revisionist Zionists, Herut, were blacklisted and shunned by mainstream Israeli society.

The Olmert family, including Ehud and his three brothers, along with other members of the Herut movement, stuck together in a neighborhood called Nahalat Jabotinsky, named after their political forefather. Perhaps because of the family's political and social isolation, Ehud grew up a staunch defender of his parents' right-wing beliefs, including a belief in the Jewish right to control all of the biblical lands of Judea, or, as the party's slogan said, "To the banks of the Jordan River," in claiming Israel's right to the whole of the West Bank.

Ehud continued his early political development with his involvement in the Betar Youth Organization. The group, a social and political group for young men and women that shared the ideology of its parent organization, Herut, was the same organization that his father had belonged to, so many years before in China. Other future conservative political leaders of Israel, including Yitzhak Shamir, Moshe Arens, and Menachem Begin rose from the ranks of the Betar Youth Organization.

Of course, belonging to Betar in the 1950s was a guaranteed path to unpopularity. As a leader of the group, Ehud and his fellow members were widely treated as outcasts. They were thought by many to be fascists for their opposition to Socialism, as well as for their dreams of an expansion of Israeli territory.

Members of Betar wore their unpopularity as a badge of achievement. As an Olmert childhood friend, Moshe Amirav,

In Ehud Olmert's early years, he absorbed his father's political views and joined the Betar Youth Organization *(above in 1942)*, a youth group dedicated to the expansion of Israel. Although it was unpopular in mainstream Israeli society, Olmert was proud to be a part of Betar and thrived on the group's message of persistence and struggle.

recalled, "We wanted to be a minority; it's in our genes." Indeed, the most valued trait in Betar was called *tagar*—persistence and struggle. As is said in the Betar hymn sung at meetings, "In the

THEY WERE SURROUNDED BY COUNTRIES THAT WANTED NOTHING MORE THAN TO SEE THEIR NATION'S DESTRUCTION.

face of every obstacle, a fire may still be lit with the flame of revolt."

Ehud Olmert has since given up on Betar's goal of an expanded "Greater Israel." But he has held on to the idea of the nobility of struggle and of the power of persistence throughout his political career.

Certainly, Ehud grew up with more than just political discussions for recreation. Like any other boy, Ehud went to school, participated in sports, and enjoyed playing with his friends. His mother, Bella, was a strict parent who made certain that Ehud always did his homework and practiced piano.

POLITICAL REVIVAL

In Israel's 1955 elections, Herut made a political comeback, doubling its number of seats in the Knesset (the Israeli legislature.) Among those winning seats in the Knesset was Ehud's father, Mordechai. Although he served as a Herut member, he refused to vote consistently as the party wanted him to and served just two terms before Menachem Begin ousted him for his stubborn independence.

He went on to head the Settlement Department of the Herut Movement, helping to establish villages and towns throughout Israel. Because of Mordechai's independence, as Gadi Taub pointed out in the *New Republic*, in many ways the Olmerts were outsiders within a community of outsiders.

But then, life in Israel was not easy for anybody. The settlers were building a new land, and they were surrounded by countries that wanted nothing more than to see their nation's destruction. And while there was no direct military action taken against Israel, the Arab countries found other ways to attack the new nation.

Beginning in the 1950s, the nations of the Arab world began a series of economic sanctions against Israel. (Many of them are still in place to this day.) Israel's neighbors all but sealed their borders to Israel, severing all forms of transportation and communication across them. The Arab world closed its ports to Israeli shipping, as well as to ships originating from or destined for Israeli ports. All flights departing from, landing in, or passing through Israel were forbidden from passing over Arab air space. Individuals who had an Israeli visa in their passport were refused entry into Arab countries. It is no wonder, then, that many Israelis felt that they were living under a constant stage of siege, threatened by enemies on all sides.

The year after Mordechai was elected to the Knesset, Israel was once again at war with its neighbor Egypt following the Suez Crisis. Relations with Egypt, which had not been good since the signing of the armistice, had gradually worsened since Gamal Abdel Nasser came to power in Egypt in 1952. By 1956, Egypt was sending guerrilla forces into Israeli territory, and Israel was launching frequent military incursions into Egyptian territory in response.

Tensions rapidly mounted when Egypt blockaded the Gulf of Aqaba and closed the Suez Canal to Israeli shipping. Egypt also nationalized the canal, claiming the right to control the canal itself, much to the fury of its longtime European controllers. In response to Egypt's moves, France and the United Kingdom (along with Israel) entered into a secret agreement to take back the canal by force.

In October of 1956, Israeli forces invaded the Gaza Strip and Sinai Peninsula. The Israeli army quickly reached the canal, and as previously agreed, French and British forces stepped in on the pretext of restoring order to a vital shipping canal.

Israeli, French, and British forces had been victorious. But because of pressure from the United States, which opposed the

When Egyptian president Gamal Abdel Nasser decided to nationalize the Suez Canal, Israel was asked to be a part of a plan to wrest control of the canal for European interests. Because Israeli forces were already attacking areas of Egypt in retaliation for Egyptian incursions on their territory, Israel readily agreed to help Britain and France and seized the Suez Canal *(above)*.

action, their armies withdrew from the canal in March 1957. Lester B. Pearson, who would later become the prime minister of Canada, had gone to the United Nations and suggested creating a United Nations Emergency Force (UNEF) in the Suez to "keep the borders at peace while a political settlement is being worked out."

The United Nations accepted this suggestion, and after several days of tense diplomacy, a neutral force not involving the United States, Britain, or France, was sent in to the area with Nasser's consent, stabilizing the area. Pearson was awarded the Nobel Peace Prize in 1957 for his efforts and is today considered to be the father of the modern concept of "peacekeeping forces."

The Suez Crisis, despite its relatively peaceful outcome, must have impressed on Ehud Olmert the importance of a strong Israeli military. Indeed, his dream was to have an illustrious and heroic military career. The time for that would come soon enough, upon his graduating from high school.

MILITARY SERVICE

A country surrounded by hostile nations, Israel calls upon all of its citizens to do their part in the nation's defense. So, like nearly every other Israeli youth, Ehud would serve time in the Israel Defense Forces (IDF), made up of the Israeli army, air force and sea corps.

The IDF was founded on May 26, 1948, after the establishment of the State of Israel, to "protect the inhabitants of Israel and to combat all forms of terrorism which threaten the daily life." The IDF succeeded the Haganah as the permanent army of the Jewish state.

National military service is compulsory for Jewish and Druze (a religious sect that broke away from mainstream Islam a thousand years ago) males over the age of 18 and Jewish women over the age of 18. Exceptions can be made on religious, physical, or psychological grounds, and there are ways to serve one's time in national service other than the military.

Men serve three years in the IDF, while women serve two, sometimes less. Women who volunteer for combat positions may need to serve for three years, due to differences in the period of training. Gay men and women also serve openly in the Israeli military and have ever since 1993.

For Ehud, a young man with obvious political aspirations, the military would be the first significant step in his career. Very few Israeli politicians have had successful careers without a successful stint in the military. And luckily for Ehud, he would be serving his time in one of Israel's most prestigious units, the Golani Brigade.

Founded on February 28, 1948, the Golani Brigade has earned a hard-fought reputation for its exceptional soldiers, its camaraderie, and its initiative. Elements of the Golani Brigade are frequently used for particularly difficult tasks where highly skilled infantry is needed. Known for their bravery, toughness, quick response, and ability to handle the hardest situation, the Golani enjoy a very high reputation among the Israeli public. For a young aspiring politician, serving in the Golani Brigade would be an auspicious beginning.

Ehud Olmert joined the 13th Regiment of the Golani Brigade in November 1963. Unfortunately for him, his military career would end soon after it began.

CHAPTER

5

War and Education

WHAT EXACTLY HAPPENED TO END HIS MILITARY CAREER (AND WHEN IT actually ended) remains somewhat unclear, but according to Ehud Olmert's own curriculum vitae,

> November 1963—Began his military service in the 13th regiment, Golani Brigade. During his service he suffered injuries to a leg and an arm, which required prolonged medical treatment.

This is all the information that is in the public record. Unable to continue in the military due to his injuries, he entered Hebrew University, majoring in philosophy, psychology, and law. (He completed his military service in 1971 working as a correspondent for the *Hamhane* newspaper.) It was during his time at Hebrew University that he became a political activist, and it was in 1966 at the age of 20 that he made his political debut.

The occasion was a political conference of the Herut Party. Much to the audience's surprise, Olmert seized the opportunity to call on Menachem Begin, the leader of Herut since the party's founding, to immediately resign. Begin, Olmert declared, had failed to lead the party to victory in national elections. It was time, he stated, for new leadership.

The crowd reacted with fury, storming the podium. According to eyewitness reports, it seems likely that he would have been physically harmed if Menachem Begin himself, who was attending the conference, had not intervened. Begin stood up between Olmert and the angry crowd and demanded that Olmert be allowed to complete his speech. According to the Israeli newspaper *Haaretz*, Begin declared, "As long as he comes to me with open demands and does not conspire against me, that is a legitimate motion."

With one speech, Ehud Olmert certainly got himself noticed. In 1967, attorney and political activist Shmuel Tamir left Herut to form the Free Center, taking Olmert along with him. Tamir would become Olmert's first political mentor. But this flurry of political activity would pale in comparison with the main event of 1967, the Six Days' War.

NEW BORDERS

Despite the state of armistice that existed between Israel and the Arab states, military tensions continued to mount through the 1950s and 1960s. Syria, aligned with the Soviet bloc, began sponsoring guerrilla raids on Israel in the early 1960s as part of its "people's war of liberation."

In 1965, the Arab states began construction of the Headwater Diversion Plan, which if completed would have greatly reduced Israel's water supply. The IDF attacked the diversion works in Syria in March, May, and August of 1965. This started a prolonged chain of border violence that led directly to the events leading to war.

In addition to sponsoring attacks against Israel (often through Jordanian territory, much to the unhappiness of Jordan's King Hussein), Syria also began shelling civilian communities in northeastern Galilee from its positions on the Golan Heights.

Palestinian guerrilla groups, especially Fatah, were also carrying out attacks on Israel, largely from bases in Syria and Jordan. As David Remnick remarked in the *New Yorker*, in the eighteen months leading up to the war, there were 120 attempts at sabotage by Palestinians, including attacks on water pumps, land mines, and skirmishes along highways. Only 11 Israelis were killed in these incidents. But, as Tom Segev pointed out in his book *1967: Israel, the War and the Year that Transformed the Middle East*, "the psychological effect . . . was far more profound than the tangible damage."

In 1966, Egypt and Syria signed a military alliance, promising that one would go to war if the other one did. Jordan joined in the alliance on May 30, 1967. At that meeting, as David Remnick pointed out in the *New Yorker*, Nasser declared that "our base objective will be the destruction of Israel." Tensions continued to mount, as did border incidents, aerial battles, and civilian deaths on both sides.

In June 1967, the united Arab military command of Egypt, Jordan, and Syria began amassing troops all along the Israeli borders. At the same time, Egypt once again closed the Straits of Tiran to Israeli shipping. Egyptian president Gamal Abdel Nasser insisted that the UNEF (the so-called peacekeeper force) leave Egypt. Despite protests from the United Nations, the United States, and most of the world community, Egyptian and Syrian forces continued to mobilize toward Israel's border.

Israel found itself torn: Should it wait for the Arab nations to attack, as they seemed to be planning to do, or should it launch a preemptive attack? Writing in 2002, National Public Radio journalist Mike Shuster expressed a view that was prevalent in Israel before the war. Many Israelis felt that the country

Surrounded by countries that saw it as a common enemy, Israel was in a precarious position after various Arab nations created an alliance against its existence. *Above*, King Hussein of Jordan *(left)* and Egyptian president Gamal Abdel Nasser *(right)* are photographed after signing a defense agreement in Cairo in June 1967.

was "surrounded by Arab states dedicated to its eradication. Egypt was ruled by Gamal Abdel Nasser, a firebrand nationalist whose army was the strongest in the Arab Middle East. Syria was governed by the radical Baathist Party, constantly issuing threats to push Israel into the sea."

Israel, faced with what it saw as provocative acts by Nasser, including the blockade of the straits and the mobilization of 100,000 troops in the Sinai, along with continuing threats by Syria and Jordan, felt it had no choice but to attack first.

On June 5, 1967, the Israeli air force launched preemptive attacks, destroying the Egyptian air force still sitting on the ground. Later the same day, the Syrian and Jordanian air forces were destroyed in the same way. Safe from air attack, Israeli military forces then defeated (almost in succession) the armies of Egypt, Jordan, and Syria. By June 11, the Arab forces were routed and all parties had accepted the cease-fire called for by UN Security Council Resolutions 235 and 236.

As a result of its stunning victory, Israel gained control of the Sinai Peninsula, the Gaza Strip, the Golan Heights, and the formerly Jordanian-controlled West Bank of the Jordan River, including East Jerusalem. In just six days, Israel had gained control of nearly all the land that the Revisionist Zionist and Herut had sought.

But it came at a price. Israel now controlled territories, particularly the Gaza Strip and the West Bank, where it would be seen by the Palestinian population as an occupier. By capturing the Sinai, the Golan Heights, and the West Bank, the Israelis had captured areas of great strategic value. At the same time, though, the West Bank alone contained over 600,000 Arabs who found themselves unwillingly living under Israeli administration.

Many Israelis hoped that the newly occupied lands could be used as part of an ongoing peace process, trading land for peace. Indeed, on November 22, 1967, the UN passed Resolution 242, calling for Israel to withdraw from the occupied territories; in return Arab states would recognize Israel's independence and right to exist and guarantee secure borders for Israel.

Unfortunately though, the Arabs and Palestinians vowed to continue fighting Israel; and Israel, understandably, refused to return the occupied territories under such conditions. Terrorist attacks and reprisals continued. For the next several years, Israel and Egypt continued to engage in artillery, sniper, and occasional air attack. This period, known as the War of Attrition, ended with cease-fire agreements, but the region remained unstable.

Unable even to begin discussing peace with its Arab neighbors, Israel solidified its position in the occupied territories by extending its military lines of defense to the boundaries of the Arab states. The Sinai, West Bank, and Golan Heights were all militarized, and parts of these areas were settled by Jewish Israelis, further enraging the resident Arab population.

It was, in essence, a mixed victory. While all Israelis were happy to have won the war, and some (including Ehud Olmert) were happy to have extended Israeli territory, there were a few who saw early on the danger of occupying lands where Israelis where not wanted. As quoted in the *New Yorker*, noted writer Amos Oz wrote in the newspaper *Davar*,

> For a month, for a year, or for a whole generation we will have to sit as occupiers in places that touch our hearts with their history. And we must remember: as occupiers, because there is no alternative. And as a pressure tactic to hasten peace. Not as saviors or liberators. Only in the twilight of myths can one speak of the liberation of a land struggling under a foreign yoke. Land is not enslaved and there is no such thing as a liberation of lands. There are enslaved people, and the word "liberation" applies only to human beings. We have not liberated Hebron and Ramallah and El-Arish, nor have we redeemed their inhabitants. We have conquered them and we are going to rule over them only until our peace is secured.

Forty years later, peace is far from being secured. Indeed, as David Remnick wrote in the *New Yorker* many years later,

> Out of it [the war], came forty years of occupation, widespread illegal settlements, the intensification of Palestinian nationalism, terrorism, counterattacks, checkpoints, failed negotiations, uprisings, and ever-deepening distrust. What great paradox of history: a war that must be won, a victory that results in a consuming misery and instability.

Every Israeli prime minister since the 1967 war, including Ehud Olmert, has had to come to terms with the consequences of the occupation.

THE LAW AND A WIFE

Although still receiving treatment for the injuries he received during his military training, Olmert took the opportunity to continue his education, graduating from Hebrew University in 1968 with a BA degree in psychology and philosophy.

Armed with his degree, he spent the next two years immersing himself in politics. Shmuel Tamir's new party, the Free Center, won four seats to the Knesset in the 1969 elections. Akiva Nof, then the secretary of the party's Knesset delegation, decided to go abroad to study. He suggested to Tamir that Olmert become his replacement. Olmert was named the party's secretary and spokesman, rapidly becoming one of Tamir's key advisors.

But for a man with Olmert's political ambitions, lacking the military credentials of most other Israeli politicians, he would have to continue his education to climb the political ladder. In 1970, he reentered Hebrew University, this time to study law.

It was a good match. With his analytical mind, studying law came easy to him, and he received his degree in just three

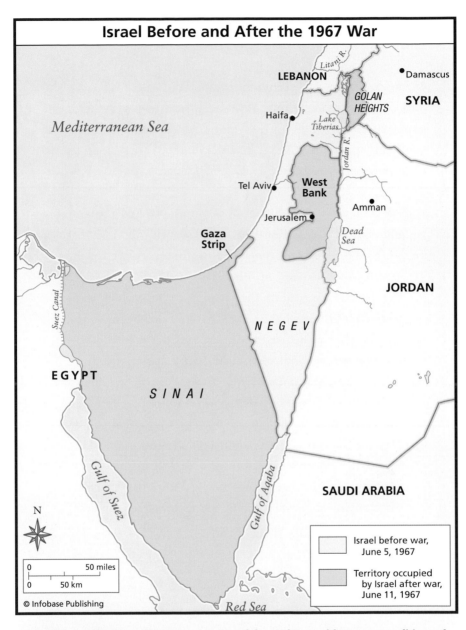

Israel Before and After the 1967 War

Despite a collective effort to erase Israel from the world map, a coalition of Middle Eastern Arab countries failed to reclaim the territory. The Six Days' War, named after the amount of time Israeli forces took to defeat Jordan, Egypt, and Syria, expanded Israel's borders to include a part of Egypt and the coveted West Bank.

years. He also left Hebrew University with something else—
a wife.

Her name was Aliza Richter. She was also a student at
Hebrew University, studying social sciences. Although she
and Ehud shared a love of Israel, they had very different
experiences growing up and stood at different ends of the
political spectrum. Aliza described the differences in an
interview with *Frontline*,

> We come from very different backgrounds. Ehud's parents
> immigrated to Israel in the early 1930s with the idea that
> we have to be strong, our task is to found a place for the
> Jewish people to live in. Ehud was raised with the idea
> that part of the country that belongs to him, which is his
> territory, was taken by the Arabs, is still ruled by the Arabs,
> and one day will be freed and given back to the Israelis—by
> force, if necessary. So that attitude, the basic attitude, at
> Ehud's house was nationalistic, it was a family of activists,
> national activists. My parents were Holocaust refugees;
> they came here in the late 1940s: all they needed and all
> they wanted was a place to put their feet on. It was kind
> of a refuge—a new place to escape to and to start a new
> life with the privilege of not being a minority anymore,
> of belonging somewhere . . . it was a completely different
> climate, you know, in our homes. We come from very
> different climates.

To Aliza, born in a camp for displaced persons in Germany
in 1946, who had immigrated to the new Jewish state in 1949,
Ehud's views *were* completely different. Her family of Holocaust
survivors was willing to give up land so that Israel could survive
and live in peace.

For Ehud Olmert and his family, compromise was out of
the question. Israel was entitled, indeed destined, to rule all

Ehud Olmert and his wife, Aliza, fell in love when they were both attending Hebrew University. Although they were from very different backgrounds and disagree on many political issues, they have a successful relationship and support each other.

SHE ADMITTED THAT UNTIL THE 2006 ELECTIONS, SHE HAD NEVER EVEN VOTED FOR HER HUSBAND.

of the land that had once been Palestine, all of the land that had been promised to the Jewish people in the Bible. They also wanted peace with their Arab neighbors, but not at the price of giving up any of the occupied territories.

And unlike Ehud, Aliza had served her full time in the IDF, working as a squad commander at Training Base 12 and as a training leader in topography. One would not naturally assume that the two would make a great match. In fact, as described in an article in the *Guardian*, initially, Aliza was not at all impressed by Ehud!

According to Amnon Dankner, a family friend and editor of the Israeli paper *Maariv* (as quoted in the *Guardian*), "She couldn't stand him at first. She remembers seeing him at some political activity, a debate or something, and he seemed too pushy." Ehud, though, was not one to give up. He followed her to the Jerusalem café where she worked, and "reluctantly, she agreed to see him," said Dankner.

While Aliza may have been initially reluctant, her reluctance soon grew into love. After just a few weeks together, the two decided to marry. As Aliza said in her *Frontline* interview, "We met at university, and we just fell in love. As simple as that. A boy meets a girl, a girl meets a boy, and that's the whole story. You don't talk ideology on those very special moments . . . We knew that we came from different backgrounds, but what the heck?"

The pairing of opposites turned into a long, loving marriage, a match of two strong-willed individuals. While Ehud mastered the art of politics, Aliza became an artist in her own right, famous throughout Israel as an artist, photographer, writer, and social worker. The plays and scripts for television she has written include "Jerusalem Between Heaven and Earth," "Fantasy for a Piano," "Panama," and "Pre-Matriculation Exam." In 2006, she published her first novel, *A Slice of Sea*. Despite her husband's success, she has always had her own life, her own causes, and her own career.

In terms of politics, she and her husband have always agreed to disagree. In fact, she admitted that until the 2006 elections, she had never even voted for her husband.

GRADUATION, POLITICS, AND ANOTHER WAR

In 1973, Olmert graduated from Hebrew University with a degree in law. Unfortunately, he had little chance to practice his new profession because in October of that year, Israel was once again at war.

The war, known as the Yom Kippur War, began on October 6, 1973 (Yom Kippur, the holy Jewish day of atonement), when Syrian and Egyptian armies launched a simultaneous surprise attack against an unprepared IDF. After initial losses during the war's first 24–48 hours, momentum shifted back toward Israel. Within three weeks the invaders were pushed back and the land was recaptured. To help keep the peace, a UN peacekeeping force was put in place.

During the war, Olmert joined the headquarters of Ariel Sharon as a military correspondent. Sharon, commanding a reserve armored division, helped locate and exploit a breach between the Egyptian forces, which ultimately turned the tide against the Egyptian army. The relationship established between Sharon and Olmert during the war would bear political fruit for Olmert in later years.

The Yom Kippur War came as a psychological and emotional shock to Israeli society. Never before had the IDF been caught off-guard. Never before had Israel come so perilously close to losing a war. In its aftermath, the Labor government began serious negotiations for security on its borders. On

January 18, 1974, a disengagement of forces agreement was signed with the Egyptian government, and on May 31 it was signed with the Syrian government.

One of the effects of the war was a growing disenchantment with the Labor Party (formerly Mapai), which had ruled Israel since its founding in 1948. In 1973, Menachem Begin, the one-time head of Herut, now Gahal, joined forces with war hero General Ariel Sharon to form a bloc of opposition parties, made up from Gahal, the Free Center Party, and other smaller parties, to create Likud ("Consolidation").

In elections held in December of 1973, the Likud won a considerable share of the votes, earning 39 seats in the Knesset. One of those seats belonged to Ehud Olmert, who, at 28, became Israel's youngest legislator. His road to power had begun.

CHAPTER

6

Climbing the Ranks

WHILE WORKING WITH SHMUEL TAMIR, EHUD OLMERT HAD AIDED HIM in investigating a number of corruption scandals. These investigations, which received some press attention, gave Olmert a reputation as a muckraker, someone who investigates and exposes problems such as political corruption, corporate crime, child labor, and other issues. Once in the Knesset, Olmert was determined to add to his reputation.

But his first full-fledged campaign against crime and corruption was not one that most people took terribly seriously. His goal? To break the grip that organized crime had on Israel's professional soccer league. Olmert, a long-time soccer fan, was determined to clean up the game.

Working with a new Labor Party MK (Member of the Knesset) named Yossi Sarid, Ehud went to work. As Sarid said, quoted in a 2006 article in *Haaretz*, "We brought a lot of joy and vitality to the petrified Knesset of the mid-1970s."

Other members of the Knesset, however, did not take the two crusaders quite as seriously. As reported in the *New Republic*, the elderly, Orthodox minister of interior, Yosef Burg, addressed the two, saying, "What organized crime? In this country nothing is organized. What makes you think crime, of all things, would be?"

But although he may have gotten off to a shaky start, Olmert's reputation as a crusader started to take shape. Working closely with journalists, Olmert helped to publicize the criminal connections of a military hero, General Rehavam Zeevy, along with corruption issues related to Avraham Ofer, the Labor minister of housing. According to the *New Republic*, he soon became known as "the investigating MK."

As Uri Blau pointed out in his article on Ehud Olmert in *Haaretz*, "Olmert's image was of a shining warrior doing battle against organized crime." Indeed, as the article described, at one point Olmert even asked the Knesset to provide him with personal security against criminals who were threatening his life.

In that speech, on December 28, 1976, MK Olmert stated from the podium of the Knesset, "I have received information that the Israel Police believe they have sufficient material to launch a criminal investigation against housing minister Ofer."

Less than a week after Olmert gave his speech, Ofer shot himself in his car. With his suicide, the investigation was closed. His son, attorney Dan Ofer, blamed Olmert for his father's death. "I accuse Ehud Olmert," he said, as quoted in *Haaretz*. "In the days preceding the suicide of my father, of blessed memory, Olmert used cheap demagoguery in the Knesset and did a character assassination of my father . . . He sought cheap publicity at the expense of my father's blood."

Despite the occasional accusation of overreaching, Olmert's investigations earned him a strong, positive reputation with the general public. He won reelection to the Knesset for seven consecutive terms, riding the wave of the ever-increasing popularity of his political party, Likud.

MENACHEM BEGIN AND THE CAMP DAVID PEACE ACCORDS

That popularity culminated in the parliamentary election held on May 17, 1977. Likud took advantage of the Israeli population's increasing disenchantment with the long-ruling Labor Party. Headed by one-time "terrorist" Menachem Begin, Likud won the election by a landslide, becoming the largest party in the Knesset.

With the party's victory, Menachem Begin became Israel's prime minister. Speaking on election night, Begin told his supporters that his victory was a "turning point in the history of the Jewish people." Little did he or his supporters know just how big a turning point his election would become.

Since 1973 and the Yom Kippur War, negotiations for Middle East peace had slowed to a near stop. Something drastic and dramatic would be needed to get everyone back to the negotiating table. In an effort to kick-start the peace process, President Anwar Sadat of Egypt did the unthinkable. On November 19, 1977, responding to an invitation from Menachem Begin, he went to Israel.

He became the first Arab leader to visit Israel, and by doing so implicitly recognized the State of Israel itself. Addressing a historic session of the Knesset, Sadat talked about his views on peace, the status of Israel's occupied territories, and the Palestinian refugee problem.

His gamble worked. After preliminary negotiations, Egyptian president Sadat and Israeli prime minister Menachem Begin agreed to meet at Camp David, Maryland, in talks to be led by U.S. president Jimmy Carter.

The talks were held September 5–17, 1978. There were numerous problems during the negotiations, and at several points both parties were willing to walk away. By all accounts, it was Jimmy Carter's relentless drive to achieve peace and his

Following in his father's footsteps, Olmert was elected to the Knesset, Israel's parliament, in 1973. As the Knesset's youngest member, he became known for his crusades to expose corruption in Israel.

reluctance to allow the two men to leave without reaching an agreement that played the decisive role in the talk's success. On March 26, 1979, the Israel-Egypt Peace Treaty was signed.

It was a milestone in modern Middle East history. There were three main features of the treaty. One, the mutual recognition of each country by the other. Two, the ending of the official state of war that had existed between the two countries since the 1948 Arab-Israeli War. And three, the withdrawal by Israel of its armed forces and civilians from the Sinai Peninsula, which Israel had occupied since the 1967 Six Days' War. It was a momentous occasion for both Israel and Egypt.

To most of the world outside of the Middle East, Anwar Sadat and Menachem Begin were heroes, and they were rewarded for their efforts with the Nobel Peace Prize. But to many in the Arab world, Anwar Sadat was a traitor who had betrayed the idea of Arab unity by reaching an agreement with Israel.

In 1979, the Arab League suspended Egypt's membership. And on October 6, 1981, Sadat was assassinated by members of the Egyptian Islamic Jihad. This organization was operating under a fatwa (religious edict on Islamic law issued by an Islamic scholar) approving the assassination from Omar Abdel-Rahman, a Muslim cleric who was later convicted in the United States for his role in the February 26, 1993, World Trade Center bombing.

Within Israel, Begin and the Camp David Accords faced opposition as well. Ironically the opposition, limited as it was, came from Begin's own party. His followers in the party found it difficult to accept that Menachem Begin, a man who had made his reputation as a proponent for the idea of a Greater Israel, would be willing to relinquish occupied territory for peace. In addition, agreeing to the forced removal of Israeli settlements and civilians from Sinai seemed to them a shocking betrayal of Likud's Revisionist ideology.

WITH THAT VOTE, OLMERT POSITIONED HIMSELF FIRMLY AS A HARD-LINE RIGHT-WINGER EVEN WITHIN LIKUD.

Several prominent Likud members, including Ariel Sharon and Yitzhak Shamir, objected to the treaty and abstained from voting. A small group of hard-liners within Likud, including Ehud Olmert, voted against the treaty, which was nonetheless ratified by an overwhelming majority.

With that vote, Olmert positioned himself firmly as a hard-line right-winger even within Likud. He was now firmly outside the mainstream of Israeli political thought. Other problems would soon arise that would further diminish his reputation.

SCANDALS

At the same time that Olmert was serving in the Knesset, Israeli law allowed him to own a private business. Thus, on the one hand he was earning a reputation as a crusader against corruption. On the other hand, he was also working as a lawyer representing the same economic interests accused of corrupting the system.

He was so successful as a lawyer that in 1978 he and two other attorneys, Uri Messer and Baruch Adler, left the offices of Jerusalem attorney Uzi Atzmon to form the law firm of Ehud Olmert and Co. It wasn't until December of 1988, when he received his first cabinet appointment by then prime minister Yitzhak Shamir, that he fully left his law practice.

Unfortunately for Olmert, accusations of somewhat less than legal dealings have followed him throughout most of his public life. Noted Israeli journalist Uri Blau wrote a magazine expose on Ehud Olmert, published in *Haaretz*. In it, he quoted Aryeh Avneri, a former reporter and chairman of Ometz, an association that fights public corruption, who has followed Olmert's career for many years.

"I wanted to understand how he managed to become rich in the course of his public activity. Olmert used to receive clients while he was an MK. People who wanted shortcuts to various authorities and bodies hired his expensive services, because of his access to Knesset committees and decision makers who dealt with the subjects they were interested in."

(It is important to remember that Olmert's outside activities as an attorney were permitted by law. Until 1996, MKs were allowed to hold other jobs in addition to their position in the Knesset. It is the way in which he used his position that is under question to this day.)

It was alleged, for example, that in 1981, Olmert received a loan of $50,000 from a fictitious company owned by the CEO of the Bank of North America. Olmert was also accused of having asked for favors on the CEO's behalf from the government's fraud investigation unit, but the Israeli attorney general at the time decided not to place Olmert on trial.

He was also implicated in a scandal involving forged receipts for donations to the 1988 Likud campaign, of which he was cotreasurer. Although three senior Likud officials were ultimately convicted, Olmert himself was acquitted. Indeed, despite facing a number of trials and investigations, Olmert has never been convicted of a crime.

Despite the fact that he has so far avoided conviction, his carefully cultivated public image as an honest crusader was damaged. He began to look just like any other wheeler-dealer politician. And, truth be told, it is hard to point a finger at someone else's corruption when one is being investigated and charged oneself.

Olmert's public image as a clean and honest politician may have taken a hit. But on a personal level, as a person and as a husband and father, nobody has ever faulted him. Many have commented on how comfortable he is with people of all walks of life, on how strong a sense of self he has, and how, unlike other politicians, he has not let his success go to his head.

In an article entitled "Ehud Olmert's Vision for Israel: Virtually Normal," published in the *New Republic,* Gadi Taub related a story that illustrates Olmert's ease with people of all social strata. In 1992, when Olmert left his position as minister of health, his staff held a small farewell party for him. People rose to tell stories about Olmert, to say farewell, and to wish him good luck:

> Amid the festivities, the cleaning woman stepped forward and asked to say a few words. In a thick Russian accent, she described how the minister would arrive early for work. She was often the only other person in the office. Every morning, for two years, he'd make coffee for her, and every morning, between 5:45 and 6:00, they would converse about their families and lives.

Like most politicians, like most people, Ehud Olmert cannot be described in simple terms of black and white, good or bad.

Throughout the late 1970s and 1980s, Olmert's career continued to rise. His family grew as well, as he and his wife, Aliza, had four biological children and adopted one child. Like many growing families, at first they had to struggle to make ends meet, moving from one apartment to another. But by the mid 1980s, Olmert was making enough money to purchase a large house located in an expensive Jerusalem neighborhood. Life for the Olmerts was definitely on the upswing.

POLITICAL CAREER

Olmert's political career, too, was definitely on the upswing as well. While still serving in the Knesset, he took on a new role, that of a member of the cabinet of then prime minister Yitzhak Shamir. From 1988 to 1990, he served as a minister without portfolio (without a formal cabinet position), handling minority affairs. From 1990 to 1992, he served as minister of health.

Ehud Olmert signs his allegiance to the state as he is sworn in as minister without portfolio *(above)*. After being appointed to the position, Olmert rose even further in the Knesset and was named health minister in 1990. His successes in that position, however, were overshadowed by the rising popularity of a rival politician, Benjamin Netanyahu.

In that position, he worked to initiate reforms that became the basis of the new national health law, which guaranteed the right of all Israeli citizens to health care. He also pressed for laws that allowed the unionization of state hospitals, giving hospital workers the right to organize and work for better working conditions.

It looked as though his slow, cautious climb through the ranks would soon pay off with even more powerful positions in government. But unfortunately for his political ambitions, the late 1980s and early 1990s saw the meteoric rise of Likud politician Benjamin Netanyahu. A new face, Netanyahu offered what seemed to be a fresh alternative to the "old party machine" of Likud, and his popularity within the party and with the general public soared.

Olmert's position with Likud was hardly strengthened by a speech he gave at a 1991 American Israel Public Affairs Committee (AIPAC) conference. (AIPAC is an American special interest group that lobbies the U.S. government in favor of maintaining a close U.S.-Israel relationship.) At that conference, Olmert said that Israel was willing to negotiate with the government of Syria on the Golan Heights. Both Shamir and Ariel Sharon subsequently denied that that was true.

Olmert's attempt to move to the left politically had failed. Feeling threatened, he decided to make a strategic retreat from the Israeli cabinet. (Olmert and Netanyahu have been fierce political rivals ever since.) Olmert instead decided to run for a new office. He decided to run for the office of mayor of Jerusalem.

Mayor and Vice Prime Minister

OLMERT'S OPPONENT IN THE RACE FOR MAYOR WAS TEDDY KOLLEK. KOLLEK, who had been mayor since 1965, was a much beloved figure in Jerusalem and widely respected around the world. His love for the city was obvious, as reflected in the following quote from the *New York Times*:

> I got into this by accident . . . I was bored. When the city was united [after the 1967 war], I saw this an historic occasion. To take care of it and show better care than anyone else ever has is a full life purpose. I think Jerusalem is the one essential element in Jewish history. A body can live without an arm or a leg, not without the heart. This is the heart and soul of it.

Olmert, too, appreciated Jerusalem's importance to the Jewish people, as is indicated from an interview for *Frontline*:

> Look, for 2,000 years Jews were praying and crying and dying to return to Jerusalem. Jerusalem, for all its history, was never a capital of any other nation but the Jewish people. All our lives, there was nothing that we prayed for or cried for more and yearned for more than to return back to Jerusalem.

Kollek was 82 and a reluctant candidate when Olmert challenged him for the position of mayor. Olmert won the election by a large margin, becoming the first Likud Party member to hold the position.

He would hold the job for two terms, until 2003, waiting patiently on the sidelines for another opportunity to try for Likud's top spot. An opportunity arose in 1999, when Olmert ran against Ariel Sharon in the Likud primaries. Losing in a landslide, Olmert continued in his position as mayor and became one of Sharon's most ardent supporters.

During his decade in the job, Olmert concentrated his efforts on improving Jerusalem's aging and crumbling infrastructure. He opened up the city to building skyscrapers and began the construction of major highways as well as a light-rail system, the first in Israel. He could point with pride to those accomplishments.

Others have pointed out the problems during his rule. To resolidify his support with the party's right-wing base after the 1991 AIPAC speech, he used considerable political capital to gain alliances with the ultra-Orthodox population of the city, a vital constituency. He spoke uncompromisingly as a member of Likud of his belief in Israel's right to Jerusalem as the undivided and eternal capital of the Jewish people, as well as of Israel's right to hold both the West Bank and the Gaza Strip.

Olmert also added to his right-wing credentials by opposing the Oslo Accords. This agreement, officially called the Declaration of Principles on Interim Self-Government

Arrangement or Declaration of Principles, called for the withdrawal of Israeli forces from parts of the Gaza Strip and the West Bank. It also affirmed a Palestinian right of self-government through the creation of the Palestinian Authority.

This agreement, finalized in Oslo, Norway, on August 20, 1993, was approved by the Israeli Knesset on September 23, 1993, by a vote of 61 to 50, with eight abstentions. And while some Palestinian groups such as Fatah accepted the accords, others, such as Hamas, the Palestinian Islamic Jihad, and the Popular Front for the Liberation of Palestine, rejected the agreement.

Despite the intentions of the accords, distrust still prevailed among both Israelis and Palestinians. Terrorist attacks against Israel by Palestinians intensified, and expansion of Israeli settlements in the occupied territories accelerated to five times its original rate.

To help solidify Israel's claim to Jerusalem, Olmert helped to strengthen Israel's control over East Jerusalem, the Arab section of the city that had been taken during the 1967 war. He did this by vigorously promoting building projects for Jews in East Jerusalem while overseeing demolition orders against Palestinian homes. To the Arab population, it seemed that Olmert was eager to push them out of the city in order to make room for Israeli Jews.

As former Palestinian legislator Hanan Ashwari said in an interview with BBC News:

> Although he [Olmert] claimed he would do more for East Jerusalem than any other mayor, that he would provide services and infrastructure and so on, he proceeded to do exactly the same if not worse.
>
> He continued land occupations, the closure of Palestinian institutions and of course [provided] no services to Palestinians. The situation deteriorated in terms of schools, roads, everything.

Even many Jewish residents of the city were disappointed in the mayor's performance. Non-religious professionals left the city in large numbers, as the city grew progressively poorer and more run-down.

Dafna Baram, news editor of *Kol Ha'ir*, a Jerusalem newspaper that ran numerous articles opposing Olmert, said about Olmert to the BBC:

> There was feeling that the city was getting uglier and uglier and the mayor wasn't interested. Ehud Olmert spent 20% of his time as mayor out of the city and, in a period where there were many bombings and the Jerusalemites felt they were suffering a lot, this was the thing that enraged our readers the most.

It wasn't only the readers of *Kol Ha'ir* who were unhappy with Olmert's position as mayor. His wife, Aliza, also disagreed with his policies, as she explained later in an interview with *Frontline*:

> When he was mayor of Jerusalem it was the hardest time for us as a couple. The level of disagreement got impossible at the times. Ehud was affiliated with the more extreme segments of society at the time. He was supporting the settlers in East Jerusalem . . . which I completely disagreed with. I thought that the only way to coexist in Jerusalem would be through compromise and through respecting their [Palestinian] rights for proper housing and proper living conditions and respecting their rights over Jerusalem, which I don't doubt.

Things got so bad, according to Aliza, that some of their friends turned their backs on them because of Ehud's policies. It took 10 years to reconcile with them.

A car bomb detonates in Jerusalem's busy Yehuda market in November 1998, killing two and injuring 21. Despite steps taken toward establishing peace among Middle Eastern nations, Israeli expansion into Palestinian territories exacerbated the situation. Olmert, who was mayor of Jerusalem at the time, responded to the attacks by increasing Jewish building projects and destroying Arab homes.

And as always, there were accusations of corruption. As the January 24, 2006, expose in *Haaretz* pointed out, Olmert's Jerusalem was "a paradise for contractors and entrepreneurs. Especially if they donated to Olmert." He was also summoned to testify in court by Yisrael Twito, an ultra-Orthodox Jew who helped Olmert in his 1993 run for mayor of Jerusalem.

Twito sued the city after his retirement as a city employee at the end of the 1990s, claiming he was still owed money. Twito claimed that Olmert had promised him a job in the municipality after the elections, but that he had sometimes been paid only an advance on his salary, and sometimes nothing at all. Olmert denied that there had been any promise of a city job in exchange for help in the election.

Nonetheless, despite the accusations, Olmert managed to raise his profile on the international stage during his years as mayor. In one instance, Olmert was an invited speaker at an international conflict resolution conference held in Derry in Northern Ireland.

In his address, quoted in the *Guardian*, he spoke of how "political leaders can help change the psychological climate which affects the quality of relationships among people." His speech concluded with reflections on the importance of the political process in overcoming differences:

> How are fears born? They are born because of differences in tradition and history; they are born because of differences in emotional, political and national circumstances. Because of such differences, people fear they cannot live together. If we are to overcome such fear, a credible and healthy process must be carefully and painfully developed. A political process that does not aim to change the other or to overcome differences, but allows each side to live peacefully in spite of their differences.

A process that would allow each side to live peacefully in spite of their differences sounds exactly like what is needed for Israel and its neighbors. And throughout the period, negotiations between the Israelis and the Palestinians continued.

In July 2000, U.S. president Bill Clinton invited Israeli prime minister Ehud Barak and Yasser Arafat, the first elected president of the Palestinian Authority, for negotiations at Camp David, Maryland. Barak, a left-wing member of the Labor Party, was ready to compromise. He offered Arafat a Palestinian state in the majority of the West Bank as well as all the Gaza Strip with an outlying suburb of East Jerusalem as its capital.

The proposal was not perfect. Israel would maintain control of some settlements and would have temporary control over 10 percent of the West Bank for an indefinite period of time (necessary, the Israelis felt, for security reasons). It was considered by most observers to be a solid basis for negotiation.

In a move widely criticized, even by members of his negotiating team and cabinet, Arafat rejected the proposal and refused to make a counteroffer. The talks broke off with no agreement in sight. Unfortunately, things would have to get even worse before there would be any hope of things getting better.

INTIFADA

In September 2000, a new wave of violence began between Palestinians and Israelis. Known as the Intifada (the Arabic word for "uprising"), it was considered by many Palestinians to be a war of national liberation against foreign occupiers (Israelis). Many Israelis, though, considered it to be nothing more than a campaign of terror.

It is also known as the Oslo War by those who consider it a result of the concessions made by the Israelis following the Oslo Accords. But whatever it is called, it is believed by most observers that the violence began on September 28, 2000, the date that Ariel Sharon visited the Temple Mount.

Sharon, then Israeli opposition leader (Labor Party leader Ehud Barak was prime minister), accompanied by a Likud

Party delegation and surrounded by hundreds of Israeli riot police, visited the mosque compound of the Temple Mount in the Old City of Jerusalem. This compound, the site of the destroyed First and Second Temples, is considered by many to be the holiest site in Judaism. It is also the third holiest site in Islam for the majority of Muslims, site of both the Dome of the Rock and Al-Aqsa Mosque. As such, it is one of the most contested religious sites in the world.

The stated purpose of Sharon's visit was to assert the right of all Israelis to visit the Temple Mount. Many critics claim, though, that Sharon knew that his visit could trigger violence and that the purpose of his visit was politically motivated.

Whatever the reason, the day after Sharon's visit, large riots broke out around Old Jerusalem. Five people were shot dead by Israeli security forces, and 200 others were wounded after Palestinians on the Temple Mount threw stones over the Western Wall at Jews and tourists below. Approximately 70 police officers were also reportedly injured in the clashes.

That same day, demonstrations and riots broke out in the West Bank. In the days that followed, demonstrations erupted throughout the West Bank and the Gaza Strip. In the West Bank city of Qalqilyah, a Palestinian police officer working with Israeli police on a joint patrol opened fire and killed his Israeli counterpart, Supt. Yosef Tabeja, an Israeli Border Police officer.

The violence quickly escalated. In the first six days of the Intifada, 61 Palestinians were killed, and 2,657 were injured by the Israeli army and police. The Intifada was in full swing. Palestinian suicide bombers worked to instill terror among the Israeli citizenry, as buses, pizza parlors, and dance clubs— anywhere large numbers of non-military civilians could be killed—were targeted.

Feeling that they were living under a constant threat, the mood of the Israeli public changed. Once optimistic that peace could be achieved through negotiation, people became pessimistic that lasting peace could ever be achieved. In the 2001 elections for prime minister, the public turned against the ruling Labor Party, electing Ariel Sharon by a decisive margin.

Because these elections were held alone, without an accompanying election for the Knesset, the Labor Party still represented the largest block in the Knesset. The result was a national unity government headed by Sharon, with eight parties united in a somewhat shaky coalition, including Labor, Likud, the National Religious Party, the National Union, and others.

Ariel Sharon, one of the heroes of the 1973 Yom Kippur War, had long been a controversial figure in Israeli politics. While seen by many as a leader who would strive to achieve peace without compromising Israel's security, others saw him as a war criminal, responsible for crimes related to the Sabra and Shatila massacres during the 1982 Lebanon War. He was a man of whom everybody had an opinion, and a man who would become Ehud Olmert's most important mentor.

Olmert was still mayor of Jerusalem, trying to govern and run a city under siege. Many terrorist attacks occurred in Jerusalem, including an attack on March 29, 2002. In that incident, 2 people were killed and 20 people were wounded when a 17-year-old suicide bomber set off her explosives in an entrance to a supermarket.

In an interview with CNN that evening, Olmert expressed his anger and outrage at the bombings, and at Yasser Arafat, who he felt controlled the Intifada.

> He has never wanted cease-fire, he never tried to cease-fire . . . He's out for Jewish blood, and he didn't make the slightest effort to stop the fire . . . On the contrary, he made all the necessary hints and signals to his people that they can continue. Suffice it to say that this morning he was calling for a million shahids to march towards Jerusalem. In other words, a million suicidal attackers to come to

The Temple Mount *(above)* has strong religious significance in both Judaism and Islam, and a right to the site is one of the most fought-over issues in Israeli-Arab relations. The visit of Ariel Sharon in 2000 initiated a burst of Palestinian-led violence against the Israeli public.

Jerusalem and to commit more and more suicidal attacks. One of them listened to him, and came already. Many more may follow suit.

In an earlier interview with CNN, on March 9, a day when at least 11 Israelis were killed and 80 were injured in two separate attacks, Olmert discussed his frustrations on the possibility of negotiating with Yasser Arafat and the Palestinian Authority:

> The bottom line is that every single day of the week . . . innocent civilians [are] being killed in their homes, in the coffee shops, in the streets or in the bars. They are just after blood, after Jewish blood, every day. No political negotiations will be meaningful, believe me. I mean, this is ridiculous. You're [saying] that the democratically elected government of the state of Israel could negotiate with Arafat, when today we had to pull out pieces of bodies from the center of Jerusalem? Do you think it is possible? Do you think that it can be done?

Despite three wars, years of military actions, and many attempts at negotiations, Israel found itself in nearly the same position it had been in since its creation—fighting to defend its citizens and borders. At the same time, the Palestinians were still fighting to gain a homeland, a state of their own. Things remained at an impasse, waiting for a new approach to peace.

MOVING ON

With the 2003 elections for the Knesset approaching, Olmert found himself at a crossroad. He had been mayor of Jerusalem for 10 years. He had learned a lot about ruling and administrating. Being mayor of Jerusalem, a city populated by many diverse ethnic and religious groups, had perhaps given him a deeper insight into the problems facing Israel. So with Israel once again facing a formidable challenge, he thought that the time was right to reenter the national political arena. He decided to once again run for a seat in the Knesset.

Not only was he running again for the Knesset, but Olmert also served as the head of the national election campaign for the Likud Party. Election Day was January 28, 2003. The Likud Party, which had run on a platform of restoring security to Israel, won a smashing victory, receiving 29.39 percent of the vote, more than doubling Labor's total. But since the party had not received a majority of the vote, a coalition government would still be necessary.

Olmert was placed in charge of those negotiations, putting together a government comprised of the Likud, Shinui, and National Union parties. (The National Religious Party joined the government on March 3.) With a ruling coalition in place, Ariel Sharon and his right-wing Likud Party were now in control.

Ehud Olmert had been elected to the Knesset, swept up in the Likud Party's victory. But he expected something more. Based on his contributions to Likud's success, as well as his own discussions with Ariel Sharon, Olmert thought that he would be rewarded with the treasury ministry, one of the most important positions he could have.

But it was not to be. In an effort to solidify his own position as head of Likud, Sharon gave the treasury to Olmert's longtime nemesis, Benjamin Netanyahu. To make up for it, Sharon offered Olmert the ministry of commerce and industry, a much less prestigious position.

At first, Olmert refused, and he briefly considered leaving government all together to work in the private sector. But Ariel Sharon respected Olmert and wanted and needed to keep him as an ally. He offered him the title of senior deputy prime minister, also known as acting prime minister, or as literally translated from the Hebrew, "Prime Minister's Place Filler."

He soon became one of Sharon's closest friends and advisors, quickly becoming known as Sharon's right-hand man.

While the position did not give Olmert much power (the position is similar, in theory at least, to that of U.S. vice president), it did place him next in line to be prime minister if Sharon should die or become incapacitated. Nobody really expected that to happen, but it proved to be enough to keep Olmert as part of Sharon's cabinet. He soon became one of Sharon's closest friends and advisors, quickly becoming known as Sharon's right-hand man. Their relationship, though, would soon be sorely tested.

OLMERT CHANGES POSITION

For months, Olmert had been pondering the following dilemma. The longer Israel held on to the occupied territories, the more Israel itself changed. The dream of a Jewish democratic state was rapidly fading as Israel was forced into the position of being a military power—an occupier of other people's lands. Thus, holding on to the territories was no longer a realistic option.

On the other hand, negotiations with the Palestinians had proved fruitless. The Palestinians themselves were unable to reach consensus on whether to negotiate with the Israelis at all. How then could Israel surrender the territories without having a reliable negotiating partner?

In December of 2003, Ehud Olmert gave an interview to Nahum Barnea of Israel's largest daily paper, *Yedioth Ahronoth*. In it, the man who had grown up with parents who had supported the idea of a Greater Israel, the man who had spent his political career defending the concept of a Greater Israel, the man who had voted against every peace treaty that Israel had ever signed, dropped a political bombshell.

He told Barnea that he favored "the unilateral evacuation of most of the territories and parts of East Jerusalem and the division of the land of Israel into two states with the border between them determined not by politics, national sentiment or religious tradition, but by demography."

In other words, since Israel was unable to negotiate with the Palestinians on the terms for withdrawing from the occupied territories, the Israelis would just pull out on their own. The headline of the article said it all, "OLMERT GETS OUT OF THE TERRITORIES." It was a politically stunning moment.

In the article, Olmert went into detail on the role that demography played in his change of opinion. He argued that Jews, given the rapidly growing Palestinian population in the occupied territories, were in danger of becoming a minority in the lands between the Jordan River and the Mediterranean Sea.

He went on to point out that Israel could not occupy the territories permanently. And since renouncing a democratic form of government was not a possibility, Israel would HAVE to leave the territories in order to save the country's soul.

According to Gadi Taub writing in the *New Republic*, Sharon was in bed with the flu when Olmert gave the interview and had no prior knowledge of what Olmert was going to say. After reading the interview in the paper, Sharon called Olmert from home.

As was later reported, Sharon spoke to his main advisor sarcastically. "Where are you," asked Sharon on the phone. "I'm home," said Olmert. "Is your home still on our side, or did you already give it to them?" asked Sharon. According to the *New Republic*, they both laughed. "In any case," Sharon said, "I'm recovering now, so you can take a break from running the state."

While Sharon may have been initially skeptical about the proposal, long discussions with Olmert may have helped push him in the direction of unilateral disengagement. Less than a month later, Ariel Sharon stunned Israel and the world by announcing that he would unilaterally move Israeli settlers and military forces out of the Gaza Strip.

The decision came at a serious political price for Olmert, Sharon, and Likud. After the *Yedioth* interview, only 7 percent of Likud members selected Olmert as their preferred candidate for prime minister. Coming out in favor of unilateral disengagement was obviously not a way to gain popularity with the right-wing members of Likud. But Olmert was convinced that he was doing the right thing, as he explained in an interview with *Frontline* in 2006.

> Yes, I have changed my opinions about some fundamental issues of our lives and I'm proud of it. Life is changing, the realities are changing, the circumstances are changing. You have to address yourself to these new changes. And inquire every day within yourself: "What should be my position about these issues now that things have changed?" and [do it] without this kind of dogmatic loyalty to your former positions because it is inconvenient or uncomfortable to show and to admit that you have changed your position.
>
> Fundamentally, I have reached a conclusion that when we have to make a choice between greater Israel or a Jewish democratic state, it is inevitable that my choice is a Jewish democratic country, and that means that we will never be able to keep all of the territories and we have to compromise on land.
>
> Now what has changed in me is my ability to spell it out explicitly—to talk about it publicly and also to lobby and push for this position because I feel that time is running out for us. I want to be in a position that I dictate the permanent solution rather than react to something that comes from the outside. I want to lead, I want to change, I want to dictate—and I'm going to do it.

A longtime supporter of Israeli politician Ariel Sharon, Olmert believed he would be rewarded for his dedication to the Likud party. Upon Sharon's election to prime minister, however, he decided to appoint Olmert to deputy prime minister, which allowed the two to work more closely together.

Olmert was also convinced that his parents, staunch believers in the concept of a Greater Israel, would have agreed with his new position. "They were practical people," he told *Frontline*. "They were absolutely dedicated to this country . . . He [my father] would have said to me, " . . . if for the sake of having territories, we compromise the Jewish democratic nature of Israel, then let's give up settlements."

Sharon, too, paid a political price within Likud. His proposal was welcomed by both the Palestinian Authority and by a clear majority of Israelis, as well as by many abroad, including the United States and the European Union. But it was greeted with opposition from within his own Likud Party and other right-wing Israelis.

Despite the opposition, Sharon pressed ahead with the plans for withdrawal from Gaza. The Knesset, on February 16, 2005, voted 59–40 (with 5 abstaining) to approve the plan. After months of political tug-of-war, Sharon's cabinet voted in August 2005 by a vote of 17–5 to approve the initial phase of withdrawals. Benjamin Netanyahu, finance minister and longtime political rival of both Olmert and Sharon, resigned in protest. Sharon promptly named Olmert to be his replacement.

Olmert took the opportunity to again voice his support of the Gaza pullout. As quoted in the *Washington Post* on August 13, Olmert said,

> I voted against Menachem Begin. I told him he made a historic mistake [regarding the 1978 Camp David Accords], how dangerous it would be, and so on and so on. Now I am sorry he is not alive for me to be able to publicly recognize his wisdom and my mistake. He was right and I was wrong. Thank God we pulled out of Sinai.

But with the Likud Party in revolt against Sharon's leadership, the Likud Central Committee refused to give final approval of Olmert's appointment. This left him in the position of *acting* finance minister, much to Sharon's frustration and personal humiliation.

The revolt within Likud continued, and on September 27, 2005, Sharon narrowly defeated a challenge to his leadership by a 52 to 48 percent vote. That move, virtually unheard of against a popular prime minister, was initiated by the Central

Committee of the Likud Party by his main rival, Benjamin Netanyahu.

Finally, Sharon had enough. He knew that Likud would never support his desire to carry out his policy of unilateral disengagement, removing Israeli settlements from Palestinian territory, and fixing Israel's borders with a prospective Palestinian state without negotiating with the Palestinians themselves if necessary. But he also knew that these policies were extremely popular with the Israeli public as a whole.

On November 21, 2005, Sharon resigned as head of Likud, announcing that he had formed a new center-left political party to be called Kadima ("Forward"). The new party would hold a place on the political spectrum between the left-wing Labor Party and the right-wing Likud. He went on to announce that he would be dissolving the Knesset, and that new parliamentary elections would be held on March 28, 2006.

Sharon's decision sent shockwaves through the Israeli political world. Ehud Olmert was one of the first to announce that he, too, would be leaving Likud and joining Kadima. Many other Likud members followed suit, and on November 30, 2005, Shimon Peres, a 60-year member of Labor and two-time prime minister, announced that he would join Kadima to help Prime Minister Sharon pursue peace with the Palestinians.

With the defection of the Sharon wing of Likud, Benjamin Netanyahu was elected his successor as leader of the party. Polls showed that Sharon was headed to an easy victory in March, and Olmert would be right there along with him, as his finance minister and top advisor. The fates, though, would have something else in mind for both Ariel Sharon and Ehud Olmert.

8

Tested

ON DECEMBER 18, 2005, ARIEL SHARON WAS HOSPITALIZED AFTER reportedly suffering a minor stroke. During his hospital stay, doctors discovered a heart ailment requiring surgery. Sharon was given orders of strict bed rest until he could have a cardiac catheterization scheduled for January 5, 2006.

Instead, Sharon returned immediately to work and suffered a massive stroke on January 4, the day before his scheduled heart surgery. After two operations lasting 7 and 14 hours, doctors stopped the bleeding in Sharon's brain but couldn't prevent him from slipping into a permanent coma. Consultations between Government Secretary Israel Maimon and Attorney General Meni Mazouz declared Sharon "temporarily incapable to carry out the duties of his office." Ehud Olmert became acting prime minister.

Given his life in politics, it seems likely that becoming prime minister had long been his goal. But it is equally unlikely that he wanted to achieve office in this way, because of someone else's illness. In an interview with *Frontline*, he explained his feelings on receiving the news.

> I got a phone call from the secretary of the cabinet, and he told me, "Mr. Olmert, I have the Attorney General on the line, and this call is taped." Of course, that was the sign that this is official and formal, and this is a constitutional act. And he said that the authorities of prime minister are bestowed upon me immediately.
>
> When I followed the news and I got more telephone calls from the hospital, I understood that life has changed, perhaps forever. That it will never be the same. My life, the country's life. This was the end of an era.

Although the circumstances were unexpected, Olmert did not display a moment's doubt that he was up to the job. He explained in the same *Frontline* interview from March 28, nearly three months after becoming acting prime minister,

> Look, in a certain way—obviously not under these circumstances—I've been practicing for this minute all my life. I've been there. I've been a minister many times. I've been mayor of the city of Jerusalem, which is perhaps in some ways more complex and more difficult than a ministerial position . . . I was vice prime minister for Sharon. So all my political life, I was moving forward to be in a position to take over one day. And this, in itself, is not something that I can't deal with. What is hard, of course, is the circumstance, which is so very unexpected.

As might be expected, the response from Aliza Olmert on hearing the news was somewhat different, as she explained in her own interview with *Frontline*:

. . . a surprise I wasn't ready for . . . our home turned into a fortress. It had been covered with green cover sheets, lots of security, lots of media around it. I remember the first thing that entered my mind is that my shabby car was standing in front of the house and saying: "Well, this is not a car of the wife of a prime minister, we should take it to the garage tomorrow." In this country, because of security measures, everything is really so dramatic. We were following the news, and the telephones were ringing, and the red telephone was installed at home and many electric wires, many sounds I haven't heard before. It was a physical manifestation of what's going to happen. I couldn't be blind to the changes any more. It's there. It's for real. So the first thing that came into my mind when we entered home was: "Bye-bye, freedom."

In that same interview, held just days before the 2006 elections, she acknowledged publicly that those elections would be the first in which she voted for her husband, saying, "I'm going to vote for him now. But it was perfectly OK with him when I didn't vote for him. It was perfectly agreed between us that we are entitled to our convictions."

She also expressed her misgivings about her husband becoming prime minister, saying, "Well, I wish that he gets what he wants, what he always wanted, even though if it was for me I would give it up. It has been imposed on me in many ways and it's not my choice . . . it's not fun at all. None of it."

But at the same time, in the same *Frontline* interview, she claimed partial credit for herself and her friends in helping to bring about Olmert's change of mind regarding the West Bank and Gaza Strip.

Ehud was influenced by his friends . . . even amongst the closest circle of friends, Ehud was a minority. Most of us think the same way. Gradually, I think he was either convinced by the arguments or he was influenced . . . it must

Olmert followed Sharon when the prime minister left the conservative Likud party to form the new, more moderate Kadima party. Unfortunately, Sharon soon suffered a debilitating stroke and was unable to lead the new political group and Israel. As acting prime minister, Olmert readily took on Sharon's responsibilities and duties, including giving a speech announcing Kadima's victory in a national election *(above)*.

make a change if your family and your friends keep pointing a finger on reality from a different angle.

Indeed, it does seem likely that Olmert's family has had an impact on the evolution of his thinking. His oldest daughter, Michal, holds a master's in psychology and leads workshops in creative thinking. Another daughter, Dana, is a lecturer in literature at Tel Aviv University and is the editor of a literature series. She is a self-identified lesbian and lives with her partner in Tel Aviv. Her parents are accepting of her sexual identity and of her partner. Dana is active in the Jerusalem branch of the Israeli human rights organization Machson Watch, a women's group that monitors alleged human rights abuses at Israeli army checkpoints. Their son Shaul married an Israeli artist and lives in New York, where he is currently an executive at Nickelodeon. After Shaul was finished with his military service, he signed a petition of the Israeli left-wing organization Yesh G'vul, urging soldiers to refuse to serve in the Palestinian territories. Another son, Ariel, lives in Paris, where he studies French literature at the Sorbonne. It is said that he did not serve in the Israeli army. Shuli is their adopted daughter, orphaned from her mother at birth.

As one might imagine, political conversations at the Olmert dinner table could be very heated, as Shaul Olmert explained in an interview with *Frontline*:

> We definitely had our share of political disagreements. I can't say that the home was divided—we agreed on some things and disagreed on others. My father always liked to say that on the most important things, meaning our favorite soccer team, there was always an agreement. When it came to politics, it wasn't always the case . . . [But] the reality is that when you live in Israel, regardless of whether or not your father is a cabinet minister or mayor or whatever he was at the time, political issues are always part of the agenda.

But as Shaul pointed out, no matter what their political disagreements, his father always supported him and the rest of the family in their choices, even when those choices have been used as a weapon by Olmert's political opponents. Take for example the following excerpt taken from a brochure distributed by right-wingers during the election campaign:

> What can we expect from a prime minister so deeply connected to the extreme left? If the sons enjoy croissants in Paris and the daughter and wife work for the Palestinians and against the Israeli army, how can father Ehud Olmert guarantee peace and security for the state?

And, despite the pressures of having a political career, Shaul praised his father's skills as a parent:

> My father is a very good father, and today he's a very good friend to me . . . His work has always been a priority, and obviously, as a younger child, it wasn't always easy for me to accept . . . Throughout time, both of us learned to accept each other as they are. I learned that he will always be devoted to his work and that there will always be other things in his life that are important, beyond the family; learning and accepting that definitely made things easier . . . [And] . . . football, or as the Americans call it, soccer, always was and always will be the most important topic of discussion at home, and there we have full compliance. We are also supportive of the exact same soccer club.

ACTING PRIME MINISTER

Initially, Olmert found himself in somewhat of an awkward position. He was now acting prime minister, with all the responsibilities that the job entailed. The man he was replacing, Ariel Sharon, was very much alive, albeit comatose. Everyone in Kadima, publicly at least, hoped and maintained that he would soon be able to return to his job. Olmert described the difficulty of the first cabinet meeting held after he'd assumed the position of prime minister in his interview with *Frontline*:

"I DIDN'T THINK THAT I HAD THE AUTHORITY . . . TO SIT IN THE CHAIR OF PRIME MINISTER SHARON."

I didn't think that I had the authority, the moral authority, and the formal authority, to sit in the chair of Prime Minister Sharon; this is his. And I think it was very important to be absolutely clear to everyone that we are waiting for him to return to his chair and that I'm not occupying his chair. I have no authority for that. And I just left it open.

I understood later, as people told me, that the sight of me sitting on the side and his chair is vacant made a certain emotional impact on people because they felt the absence without words, without saying anything; it was made so clear and so powerful that he is absent and we all miss him.

But although Olmert may have missed Sharon, he did not hesitate to let the country know that he was now in charge. Olmert and the cabinet announced that the elections would take place on March 28 as scheduled.

In the days following Sharon's stroke, Olmert met with Shimon Peres and other Sharon supporters. To maintain his position, he would need to convince them to stay with Kadima rather than return to Likud or, in the case of Peres, Labor. Peres announced his support for Olmert, and other Kadima members fell into line. On January 16, 2006, Olmert was elected acting chairman of Kadima and the number one candidate in the March 28 elections.

In his first major policy address as acting prime minister, Olmert said at the Herzliya conference on January 24 that he backed the creation of a Palestinian state and that Israel would have to give up parts of the West Bank in order to maintain its Jewish majority within Israel. (If Israel held on to the West Bank, the Arab population would soon outnumber the Jewish population, and Israel would no longer be a Jewish state, especially if the Palestinian Arabs were given the vote.)

At the same time he said, as quoted on the Israeli Embassy Web site (http://www.israelemb.org), "We firmly stand by the historic right of the people of Israel to the entire Land of Israel. Every hill in Samaria and every valley in Judea is part of our historic homeland. We do not forget this, not even for one moment. However, the choice between the desire to allow every Jew to live anywhere in the Land of Israel to the existence of the State of Israel as a Jewish country—obligates relinquishing parts of the Land of Israel. This is not a relinquishing of the Zionist idea, rather the essential realization—of the Zionist goal—ensuring the existence of a Jewish and democratic state in the Land of Israel."

ELECTIONS

As the election campaign began, polls showed a sizeable lead for Kadima, demonstrating perhaps that the Israeli public was in favor of the party's ideology and platform, despite Sharon's absence. But then there came a shock, which some thought might lead to a collapse of Kadima's popularity.

On January 25, 2006, elections were held for the Palestinian Legislative Council, the legislature of the Palestinian National Authority (PNA), in the Gaza Strip and West Bank. To the surprise of many, the ruling party, Fatah, was soundly defeated by Hamas, which won 74 seats to Fatah's 45, providing Hamas a majority of the seats.

Hamas is a Palestinian Sunni militant organization, best known in the West and in Israel for its suicide bombings and other attacks directed against civilians and Israeli military and security forces targets. Hamas's charter (written in 1988 and still in effect) calls for the destruction of the State of Israel and its replacement with a Palestinian Islamic state in the area that is now Israel, the West Bank, and the Gaza Strip.

Many observers felt that with the election of Hamas, voters might shy away from the concept of unilateral withdrawal and

Hamas supporters celebrate their victory in the general election in 2006. When the militant group won control of the Palestinian Legislative Council, many believed it would cause even further delays in establishing peace in the region. Labeled a terrorist organization by Israel and the European Union, Hamas has many supporters and is said to be responsible for organizing attacks and suicide bombings against the Jewish state.

vote for the Likud. Instead, the public took it as proof that the Palestinians would not sign a peace deal. With no negotiating partner to work with, it would be up to Israel to take measures on its own to establish permanent and secure borders.

On Election Day, although the polls had predicted a larger victory for Kadima, the newly formed party won the largest block of seats, 29, in the Knesset. A jubilant Ehud Olmert spoke to party members after the vote, saying, "Israel wants to move forward, wants Kadima. In this moment, at the end of the battle, we return to be one people, a united people." He also promised to make Israel a just, strong, peaceful, and prosperous state, respecting the rights of minorities; cherishing education, culture, and science; and above all, striving to achieve lasting peace with the Palestinians.

The president of Israel, Moshe Katsav, formally asked Olmert on April 6 to form a government, making him prime minister designate. Olmert had an initial period of 28 days to form a governing coalition. On April 11, 2006, the Israeli cabinet deemed that Sharon was incapacitated. The 100-day replacement deadline was extended due to the Jewish festival of Passover. An additional provision was made that should Sharon's condition improve between April 11 and April 14, the declaration would not take effect.

Therefore, it was on April 14 that the official declaration was made, formally ending Sharon's term as prime minister and making Olmert the country's new prime minister. On May 4, 2006, Olmert presented his new government to the Knesset. Olmert became prime minister and minister for welfare. He was now officially prime minister in his own right.

Three weeks later, on May 24, Olmert was invited to address a joint session of the U.S. Congress, the third Israeli prime minister to do so. In his address, he spoke of his parents, their dreams, and of Israel's suffering:

> My parents Bella and Mordechai Olmert were lucky . . . they escaped the persecution in Ukraine and Russia and found sanctuary in Harbin, China. They immigrated to Israel to fulfill their dream of building a Jewish and democratic state living in peace in the land of our ancestors . . . Distinguished members of Congress, I come here—to this land of home of liberty and democracy—to tell you that my parents' dream, our dream has only been partly fulfilled. We have

succeeded in building a Jewish democratic homeland. We have succeeded in creating an oasis of hope and opportunity in a troubled region. But there has not been one year . . . one week . . . even one day . . . of peace in our tortured land . . . Over the past six years more than 20,000 attempted terrorist attacks have been initiated against the people of Israel. Most, thankfully, have been foiled by our security forces. But those which have succeeded have resulted in the deaths of hundreds of innocent civilians . . . and the injury of thousands—many of them children guilty ONLY of being in what proved to be the wrong place at the wrong time.

He went on to pledge that his government would proceed with Israel's unilateral disengagement plan if it could not come to agreement with the Palestinians. Peace was the ultimate goal, he said, adding that, "With the vision of Ariel Sharon guiding my actions, from this podium today, I extend my hand in peace to Mahmoud Abbas, elected President of the Palestinian Authority. On behalf of the State of Israel, we are willing to negotiate with the Palestinian Authority . . . The goal is to break the chains that have tangled our two people in unrelenting violence for far too many generations. With our futures unbound peace and stability might finally find its way to the doorsteps of this troubled region."

Ehud Olmert was ready to attempt to reach an agreement with the Palestinians. But sometimes history has other plans. As summer turned to fall in 2006, tensions mounted along the Israeli–Lebanese border.

9

Lebanon

ALMOST FROM ISRAEL'S BEGINNINGS AS A NATION, THERE HAVE BEEN military clashes involving Israel, Lebanon, and various independently operating militias acting from within Lebanon.

The Palestine Liberation Organization (PLO) recruited militants in Lebanon from the families of Palestinian refugees who had left Israel in 1948. By 1968, the PLO and Israel were attacking each other across the border in violation of Lebanese sovereignty. After the PLO leadership and its Fatah brigade were expelled from Jordan, they entered Lebanon and the cross-border violence increased. In the meanwhile, tensions within Lebanon erupted into the Lebanese Civil War (1975–1990).

Israel invaded Lebanon in 1978 in an attempt to stop the Palestinian attacks. (During this time, Ehud Olmert volunteered for reserve service in Lebanon.) Israel invaded Lebanon again in 1982, forcefully expelling the PLO. Israel withdrew to a slim borderland buffer zone, which it held with the aid of proxy militants in the South Lebanon Army (SLA).

In 1985, a Lebanese Shiite resistance movement, sponsored by Iran, that called itself Hezbollah, called for armed struggle to end the Israeli occupation of Lebanese territory. When the Lebanese Civil War finally ended, most warring factions agreed to put down their arms, but Hezbollah and the SLA refused. Continuous fighting with Hezbollah weakened Israeli resolve to hold on to the buffer zone, and with the collapse of the SLA, the Israelis withdrew from Lebanon in 2000 to their side of the United Nation–designated border.

In the 2000 parliamentary elections in Lebanon, Hezbollah, aligned with the Amal movement, won all 23 seats allotted for south Lebanon. Thus, while Hezbollah remained an independent armed resistance movement, it was also a part of the Lebanese government.

Citing Israeli control of the Shebaa Farms territory, Hezbollah continued to attack across the Israeli border over the next six years. (Israel had captured Shebaa Farms from Syria during the Six Days' War, along with the Golan Heights. The territory itself is in some dispute. When Israel withdrew its forces from Lebanon, both Lebanon and Syria claimed the withdrawal was incomplete, saying that Shebaa Farms was actually part of Lebanon. Israel disagrees.)

One of Hezbollah's new goals was to obtain freedom for Lebanese citizens held in Israeli prisons, and indeed, it used the tactic of capturing Israeli soldiers as leverage for a prisoner exchange in 2004. This was just a prelude to the events of summer and fall 2006.

2006 LEBANON WAR

On May 26, 2006, a car bomb killed Palestinian Islamic Jihad leader Mahmoud Majzoub and his brother in the Lebanese city of Sidon. Lebanese prime minister Fuad Siniora called Israel the prime suspect, but Israel denied involvement. Two days

In 2006, tensions between Lebanon and Israel triggered an all-out war between the two countries. Hezbollah, a militant group that held parliamentary seats in Lebanon, retaliated violently when Israeli airstrikes near their headquarters destroyed entire neighborhoods, such as the Beirut suburb *above*.

later, rockets were fired from Lebanon into Israel. Hours later, Israel responded by bombing suspected militant rocket launch sites and exchanging fire across the border. The United Nations negotiated a cease-fire the same day.

Despite the cease-fire, tensions remained high. On July 12, 2006, in what is known as the Zar'it-Shtula incident, Hezbollah launched diversionary rocket attacks onto Israeli military positions near the coast and near the Israeli border village of Zar'it.

At the same time, another Hezbollah group crossed the border from Lebanon into Israel and ambushed two Israeli army vehicles, killing three Israeli soldiers and seizing two others. (It was the second time in three weeks that an Israeli soldier had been abducted. On June 25, Israeli army Cpl. Gilad Shalit was abducted in Gaza, triggering a military offensive by the IDF.)

Hezbollah demanded the release of Lebanese prisoners held by Israel in exchange for the captured soldiers, saying, as quoted on CNN, that the abductions were "our natural, only and logical right." Israel rebuffed the Lebanese demand, saying that a prisoner exchange would only serve to encourage additional kidnappings. The Israeli cabinet authorized "severe and harsh" retaliation against Lebanon for its role in the raid.

Olmert also accused the Lebanese government, not just the Hezbollah militia, of complicity in the kidnappings. As quoted on CNN, Olmert said that the raid was "not a terror attack, but an operation of a sovereign state without any reason or provocation. The Lebanese government, which Hezbollah is part of, is trying to undermine the stability of the region, and the Lebanese government will be responsible for the consequences."

Olmert called Lebanon's actions, as quoted in the *Guardian*, "an act of war." Israel blamed the Lebanese government for the raid because it was carried out from Lebanese territory and because Hezbollah had two ministers serving in the Lebanese cabinet at that time. But the Lebanese government denied responsibility, with Prime Minister Siniora denying any knowledge of the raid and stating that he did not condone it.

Heavy fire between the two sides was exchanged along the length of the Blue Line, with Hezbollah targeting IDF positions near Israeli towns, beginning the 2006 Lebanon War. Israel responded with massive air strikes (over 12,000 combat missions) and artillery fire on targets throughout Lebanon, an air and naval blockade, and a ground invasion of southern Lebanon.

During the campaign, Hezbollah fired approximately 4,000 rockets into northern Israel. Of these, approximately 23 percent hit built-up areas, primarily civilian in nature. Hezbollah also engaged in guerrilla warfare with the IDF, attacking from surprisingly well-fortified positions. These attacks by small, well-armed units caused serious problems for the IDF.

Indeed, much to the surprise of many who expected an easy victory against an unorganized terrorist organization, Hezbollah turned out to be, as described by the Israeli newspaper *Haaretz*, a trained, skilled, well-organized, and highly motivated infantry that was equipped with the cream of modern weaponry from the arsenals of Syria, Iran, Russia, and China.

Despite this, much of the world's popular opinion turned against the Israelis. The *Times* of London asked Olmert about this in an interview, asking him, "there is a sense in the world, and you must be aware of it, of lack of 'proportionality.' Many people question how after two soldiers kidnapped and eight killed by Hezbollah we are now seeing upwards of 400 dead and rising in Lebanon. How can such in initial incident justify such a huge response from Israel?" Olmert replied:

"WHEN WE KILL INNOCENT PEOPLE WE CONSIDER IT A FAILURE, WHEN THEY KILL INNOCENT PEOPLE THEY CONSIDER IT A SUCCESS."

I think that you are missing a major part. The war started not only by killing eight Israeli soldiers and abducting two but by shooting Katyusha and other rockets on the northern cities of Israel on that same morning. Indiscrimately.

Now we know that for years Hezbollah—assisted by Iran—built an infrastructure of a very significant volume in the south part of Lebanon to be used against Israeli people. The most obvious, simple, way to describe it to the average British person is: can you imagine seven million British citizens sitting for 22 days in Manchester, Liverpool, Birmingham, in Newcastle, in Brighton and in other cities? Twenty-two days in shelters because a terrorist organization was shooting rockets and missiles on their heads? What would have been the British response to that? Do you know of a country that would have responded to such a brutal attack on its citizens softer than Israel did?

What are we talking about? More than a million Israelis are sitting 22 days in shelters because of the fear of terrorists. In every single case . . . that we kill an uninvolved civilian in Lebanon, we consider it a failure for Israel . . . The difference between us and Hezbollah is that when we kill innocent people we consider it a failure, when they kill innocent people they consider it a success.

Pressure built on both sides to bring the war to an end. Hezbollah maintained the need for an unconditional cease-fire, but Israel insisted upon a conditional cease-fire, including the return of the two abducted soldiers.

Lebanon frequently asked the United Nations Security Council to call for an immediate, unconditional cease-fire, but the United States and the United Kingdom, hoping that Israel would be able to destroy Hezbollah, interfered in the cease-fire process. Only when it became evident that Hezbollah would not easily be defeated did those countries allow the cease-fire process to proceed.

On August 11, 2006, the United Nations Security Council unanimously approved UN Security Council Resolution 1701, attempting to end the hostilities. It was accepted by the Lebanese government and Hezbollah on August 12, and by the Israeli government on August 13. The cease-fire went into effect on August 14, 2006.

AFTERMATH

The war killed more than 1,500 people, mostly Lebanese civilians. It severely damaged Lebanon's infrastructure and displaced nearly one million Lebanese and half a million Israelis. A disaster for both Lebanon and Israel, it also left Ehud Olmert's political career in shambles and Olmert himself fighting for his political future.

Olmert tried to argue that Israel had, in fact, won the war, telling the *Times* just weeks before the cease-fire that,

> I think that the military campaign had been brilliant . . . I think that in the long run this is a dramatic defeat for Hezbollah and for the Iranians that manipulated them. I think the Iranians as well as Hezbollah made a dramatic error of judgment, which is the source of all this failure. And this error of judgment was that Israel would not respond in the way that we did.

To most observers though, as well as to the Israeli public, the war had been a defeat for Israel. The country had not been able to defeat Hezbollah, had lost prestige in the world community, and had not even been able to free the two soldiers whose

The Lebanese-Israeli War displaced millions of Lebanese and Israeli citizens and caused extensive damage to Lebanon's infrastructure. *Above*, in August 2006, Lebanese citizens attempt to return to their homes over damaged roads and ruined bridges after the conflict.

kidnapping had helped trigger the war in the first place. (To this date, the two men are still being held in Lebanon.) Unhappy with the results of the war, the public turned on Olmert.

On August 21, just one week after the cease-fire, a group of demobilized Israeli reserve soldiers along with parents of soldiers killed in the fighting started a movement calling for the resignation of Ehud Olmert and the establishment of a state commission of inquiry. They set up a protest tent opposite the Knesset and grew to over 2,000 supporters by August 25.

As the public outcry mounted, Olmert announced that there would be two internal inspection probes but no independent state or governmental commission of inquiry. Critics exploded in anger, arguing that the committees would be powerless to do a truly unbiased investigation.

Due to these additional pressures, on October 11, the probe was elevated to the status of governmental commission: the Winograd Commission, headed by retired justice Eliyahu Winograd. The commission would have all the investigative powers that Olmert's critics had called for.

Just before Yom Kippur, an unsigned ad was placed in the newspaper *Maariv* by the movement to force Prime Minister Olmert out of office. As cited in the *New Republic*, the ad said, "Olmert, we forgive you. We forgive you for the first defeat in war since the founding of the state of Israel. We forgive you for the penetration of corruption into government. We forgive you for the confused leadership. We forgive you because the job is simply too big for you."

In the meantime, Olmert's popularity continued to plummet. From an approval rating of 93 percent during the war, it plummeted to as low as just 2 percent in some polls. Most wondered just how long he could manage to hold on as prime minister. As 2006 came to an end, it seemed unlikely that he would be able to last out his term.

CHAPTER

10

The End of His Political Career?

THOSE WHO THOUGHT THAT EHUD OLMERT WOULD QUIETLY RESIGN HIS post did not know him very well. As a leader of the Betar Youth Movement, he knew what it was like to be a political outcast. And he knew how to persevere. If Olmert was going to go down, it wasn't going to be without a fight. He had a job to do—a job that he had been elected to do, and he was going to do it.

For example, on September 26, 2006, just a little more than a month after the war in Lebanon ended, the BBC reported that Olmert had held a meeting with a senior member of the Saudi royal family. These talks reportedly included a Saudi proposal to lead Arab states to recognize Israel's right to exist, in exchange for Israel removing its forces from the occupied territories.

On December 8 of the same year, Olmert met with Russian president Vladimir Putin to discuss Iran's nuclear program. He told Putin that he hoped the United Nations Security Council would vote to impose sanctions against Iran if Iran continued to ignore the international community's demands that it stop its program of nuclear development.

It was going to be a struggle to win back the affection of the Israeli public. As Gregory Levey pointed out in a July 3, 2007, article posted on Salon.com,

> Since he took over for Ariel Sharon in January 2006, there have been the election of the militant Hamas government, a total breakdown in the peace process, the kidnapping of Israeli soldiers, a barrage of rocket attacks on Israeli cities, rising tensions with Iran, and last summer's disastrous war with the Hezbollah, for which Olmert was later brutally criticized by a government commission. His detractors emphasize that Olmert failed to secure the release of the kidnapped Israeli soldiers and crush Hezbollah, and that he has failed to make any progress toward an agreement with the Palestinians. The Israeli public appears to have overwhelmingly lost faith in his leadership; a recent poll showed his public approval rating at a mere 3 percent, absurdly low even in Israeli politics.
>
> It's not surprising, then, that foreign and Israeli observers have been predicting the imminent demise of the Olmert government for some time now, and it may indeed seem that he is hanging on to power by the thinnest of threads.

To the surprise of many, he *has* held on. Not bowing in the face of adversity, Olmert has made the changes necessary to, as Gregory Levey predicted, "lock down his position in the prime minister's office until at least [2008], which, on the Israeli political timescale, is an eternity."

For example, on June 18, 2006, former prime minister Ehud Barak was appointed as the new defense minister, replacing Amir Peretz, whose reputation had been badly damaged by the Winograd Report. Barak, the former chief of staff in the military and the most decorated officer in the history of Israel,

Losing the war with Lebanon was one of the many blows to Olmert's reputation and government. Unhappy with his lack of progress and success in establishing peace among the Middle Eastern countries, Israelis protested and called for an investigation into the government's actions during the war. *Above*, Israeli reservist soldiers protest outside Olmert's office in August 2006.

added an image of strength and impeccable military credentials to a badly damaged administration.

And, on July 15, 2007, Shimon Peres became Israel's new president. In Israel, the presidency is a largely symbolic position, but one with a great deal of visibility. Peres, like Barak, is a friend of Olmert and is also a member of Kadima. Peres' election to the presidency is considered by many a political victory for Olmert.

Because of the high esteem in which Peres is held throughout the world, it seems likely that he will serve as a global diplomat for Olmert, working to gain support for Olmert's diplomatic policies throughout Europe, the United States, and even in the Arab world. As Gregory Levey noted in his Salon.com article, many Israeli political commentators have called the victories of Barak and Peres the dawning of a "second Olmert government."

Even the political turmoil in the Gaza Strip may ironically have helped to strengthen Olmert's position. There, in June of 2007, the Palestinian Civil War between Hamas and Fatah intensified. Hamas defeated Fatah, and by June 14, 2007, the Gaza Strip was completely overtaken by Hamas, resulting in a Gaza Strip government that maintains that it is the legitimate government of the Palestinian National Authority. Retaliation by Fatah against Hamas in the West Bank has led to the opposite result there, with Fatah claiming to be the sole legitimate government.

Hamas was now running what seems to many to be nothing more than a failed state, making it easy for Olmert to make the political argument that it is impossible at the present time to negotiate with the Palestinians. In turn, this gives him the ability to resist outside pressure, largely from the U.S. State Department, to reach an agreement, as well as to strengthen his position within the Israeli right wing by NOT negotiating with Hamas.

Levey pointed out that in many ways, Olmert seems to have learned from his political mentor Ariel Sharon, who was "a master at political maneuvering and holding on to power." Olmert has become less open to the media and less straightforward in his statements when he does make public comments. By making it harder to know what exactly he is thinking and planning, it makes it more difficult for his political enemies to attack him.

Olmert has become less open to the media and less straightforward in his statements when he does make public comments.

Even though he seems to have weathered the worst of the fallout from the Lebanon War, things could change in an instant. There could be another war with Hezbollah. War could break out with another country, perhaps Syria, as some analysts predict.

And, as Yossi Klein Halevi noted in the *New Republic*, Olmert may soon face one of the most fateful decisions any Israeli prime minister has had to face. If Iran should continue in its drive to build nuclear weapons and the United States is unable to stop it, what should Israel do?

Can Israel take the risk of allowing Iran, a nation that has questioned Israel's right to exist as a Jewish state, to have nuclear weapons? Or should it preemptively bomb Iran's nuclear facilities and risk retaliation by Iranian ballistic missiles? However the question is resolved will have major ramifications throughout Middle East politics.

UPS AND DOWNS

Olmert avoided more political damage when the Winograd Commission released it's final report on the 2006 War in Lebanon on January 30, 2008. To the surprise of many, the report was far less critical of Olmert than in its interim report, arguing that even though critical mistakes had been made in the way the war was handled that "We are persuaded that both the prime minister and the defense minister operated out of a strong and honest assessment and understanding of what, to them, was seen as necessary for Israel's interests."

With that potential landmine avoided, Olmert began to concentrate on a final push for a peace accord between Israel

While Olmert's term as prime minister has not been exceptional, his plans to initiate further discussions with neighboring Arab nations regarding peace in the region remain hopeful. In July 2008, Olmert announced his intention to resign from office, making Israel's future uncertain.

and the Palestinians. Under the prodding of the United States and President George W. Bush, who expressed a desire for a resolution of the Palestinian problem by the end of 2008, negotiations began between both sides for the first time in seven years. By May 2008, there were reports that Olmert and Palestinian Authority President Mahmoud Abbas were close to a statement of principles that could serve as a document for both sides to ratify on the outlines of a peace treaty.

At the same time though, Olmert found himself once again on-the-ropes politically when it became public that he was the subject of yet another police investigation regarding allegations of bribery. Accused of taking bribes from Jewish-American business man Morris Talansky when he was running for Mayor of Jerusalem, leadership of the Likud and candidacy in the Likud list for the Knesset, Olmert resisted the immediate calls for him to resign, and said in a national address, quoted at CNN.com that "I am looking all of you in the eye, and I say that I never took bribes; I never took a cent for myself," before going on to say that if indicted he would, indeed resign.

On May 23, 2008, Olmert was interrogated by National Fraud Squad investigators. On May 27, 2008, Morris Talanaky testifed in front of court that over the last 15 years he had given Olmert more than $150,000 in cash in envelopes. This was the fifth such probe since Olmert had become prime minister.

In July 2008, Olmert announced his plans to resign from office once his party has elected a new leader. In his resignation speech, Olmert explained, "The entire time I was forced to defend myself from ceaseless attacks by the self-appointed soldiers of justice, who sought to oust me from my position. I am the prime minister, and am naturally a target for political struggle. But every intelligent person knows that things are totally out of proportion. Have I made mistakes in my many years of political activity? Of course! I am sorry and regret them. But is the true picture of things the one that is presented to the public? Not at all!"

Waiting on the sidelines is Olmert's defense minister, Ehud Barak. It is no secret in Israel that Barak would like to become Israel's prime minister again. No matter what happens, Olmert's career in Israeli politics will not be forgotten. A crusader accused of corruption, a career politician whose wife and children have disapproved of his politics, a right-winger who came to the realization that Israel could not hold on to the occupied territories—he is a contradictory figure. But most of all, Ehud Olmert is his parents' child.

Mordechai and Bella Olmert devoted their lives to the establishment of a democratic Jewish state. As Ehud Olmert said in his address to the U.S. Congress on May 24, 2006,

> My parents came to the Holy Land following a verse in the Old Testament in the book of second Samuel, "I will appoint a place for my people Israel and I will plant them in their land and they will dwell in their own place and be disturbed no more."

That dream, of a homeland where the Jewish people could live in peace, has become a partial reality. The homeland is there, thanks to the contributions of people like Mordechai and Bella Olmert. Their son Ehud has spent his lifetime helping to ensure that Israel will become a land where the Jewish people could live in peace and "be disturbed no more."

CHRONOLOGY

A.D. 70– **A.D. 135**	Revolts against the Roman Empire in Judea lead to the expulsion of Jews from Jerusalem and the beginning of the Jewish Diaspora, the dispersal of Jews from their traditional homeland. Roman emperor Hadrian changes the name of Judea to "Syria Palaestina."
13th–19th **centuries**	The aliyah, the return of Jews to the land of Israel, slowly begins.
1897	The First Zionist Congress proclaims the decision "to establish a home for the Jewish people in Eretz Yisrael secured under public law."
Early 20th century	Jewish immigration into Palestine continues.
1917	The British issue the Balfour Declaration, calling for the establishment of a national home for the Jewish people in Palestine.
1939–1945	World War II. In 1939, the British issue the MacDonald White Paper, limiting Jewish immigration into Palestine.
1945	**September 20** Ehud Olmert is born in the city of Binyamina, Palestine.
1945–1947	The world learns of the Holocaust, Hitler's attempt to exterminate the Jews of Europe. With six million Jews dead, pressure mounts for the establishment of a Jewish state.
1947	**November 28** The United Nations approves a plan for partitioning Palestine into three parts: a Jewish state, an Arab state, and an International Zone to administrate Jerusalem and the surrounding area.

1948   **May 14** The State of Israel declares itself an independent nation. It is immediately attacked by the armed forces of Syria, Iraq, Transjordan, Lebanon, and Egypt. Israel repulses the invaders and captures half of the territory designated for the Arab state.

1956   **October** The Suez Crisis. After Egypt blockades the Gulf of Aqaba, nationalizes the Suez Canal, and closes the canal to Israeli shipping, Israeli forces invade the Gaza Strip and Sinai Peninsula with the support of the British and the French. Israeli forces withdraw from the canal in March 1957 under U.S. pressure.

1963   **November** Ehud Olmert joins the Israeli Defense Forces in the Golani Brigade. During his service he suffers injuries to his leg and arm, requiring prolonged medical treatment. Because of his injuries, he is unable to complete his military service.

1965–1968   Olmert attends Hebrew University, receiving his BA degree in psychology and philosophy.

1967   **June** The Six Days' War. Faced with Egyptian, Syrian, and Jordanian forces massed on its borders, Israel launches a preemptive attack on June 5, destroying all enemy air forces on the ground. By the time a cease-fire is accepted on June 11, the Arab forces are routed, and Israel has gained control of the Sinai Peninsula, the Gaza Strip, the Golan Heights, and the Jordanian-controlled West Bank of the Jordan River, including East Jerusalem.

1970–1973   Olmert attends Hebrew University, receiving a BA degree in law. Marries Aliza Richter.

| 1973 | **October** The Yom Kippur War. In a surprise attack, Egyptian and Syrian armed forces attack Israel. After initial losses, the war's momentum shifts back to Israel. |

1973   **October** The Yom Kippur War. In a surprise attack, Egyptian and Syrian armed forces attack Israel. After initial losses, the war's momentum shifts back to Israel.

1973   **December** Ehud Olmert is elected to the Knesset. He will win reelection seven times.

1977   **November 19** Anwar Sadat flies to Israel, becoming the first Arab leader to visit the nation since independence. His initiative will open the way to peace talks between Egypt and Israel.

1979   **March 26** The Israel-Egypt Peace Treaty is signed. Olmert votes against it.

1988–1990   Ehud Olmert serves as minister without portfolio (without a formal cabinet position) handling minority affairs.

1990–1992   Olmert serves as minister of health.

1993   Faced with the growing popularity of rival Likud Party member Benjamin Netanyahu, Olmert leaves the cabinet and runs for mayor of Jerusalem. He will serve two terms, serving until 2003.

2000   Beginning of Intifada, a new wave of violence between Palestinians and Israelis.

2003   Olmert runs for Knesset and wins. He joins the cabinet of the new prime minister Ariel Sharon, accepting the positions of minister of commerce and industry, as well as of senior deputy prime minister, placing him next in the line of succession should Sharon be unable to serve as prime minister.

2003   **December** Olmert gives an interview with Nahum Barnea of *Yedioth Ahronoth*, calling for the unilateral evacuation of most of the occupied territories and parts of East Jerusalem. Less than a month later, Ariel Sharon announces that Israel will unilaterally move out of the Gaza Strip.

2005   **November 21**   Faced with dissent within Likud over the withdrawal from Gaza, Ariel Sharon announces that he is leaving Likud to form a new political party, to be called Kadima. Olmert announces that he will join the new party. New elections are to be held on March 28, 2006.

2006   **January 4**   Prime Minister Ariel Sharon suffers a massive stroke and goes into a permanent coma. Ehud Olmert becomes acting prime minister.

2006   **March 28**   Elections are held, and Kadima wins 29 seats, the largest block in the Knesset.

2006   **April 14**   Ehud Olmert becomes Israel's new prime minister.

2006   **July–August**   2006 Lebanon War. Israeli troops battle Hezbollah in Lebanon and northern Israel. During the war, Hezbollah fires 4,000 rockets into northern Israel, largely targeting civilians. The war comes to an indecisive conclusion on August 14. Bowing to public, pressure Olmert launches a commission to investigate the events leading up to the war and to examine how the war itself was carried out.

2007   **April 30**   The Winograd Commission issues its preliminary report, accusing Olmert of "a serious failure in exercising judgment, responsibility, and prudence."According to some polls, Olmert's popularity is as low as 2 percent. Many wonder how long he will be able to hold on to his position of prime minister.

BIBLIOGRAPHY

Bikel, Ofra. "Interview with Aliza Olmert." *Frontline/World.* PBS.org. March 28, 2006. Available online. http://www.pbs.org/frontlineworld/stories/israel502/interviews_aliza.html.

Bikel, Ofra. "Interview with Ehud Olmert." *Frontline/World.* PBS.org. March 28, 2006. Available online. http://www.pbs.org/frontlineworld/stories/israel502/interviews_olmert.html.

Bikel, Ofra. "Interview with Shaul Olmert." *Frontline/World.* PBS.org. March 28, 2006. Available online. http://www.pbs.org/frontlineworld/stories/israel502/interviews_shaul.html.

"Biography of Ehud Olmert." Zionism and Israel Information Center. Available online. http://www.zionism-israel.com/bio/Olmert_biography.htm.

Blau, Uri. "Haaretz Magazine Expose on Ehud Olmert: With a Little Help from His Friends." IMRA.org. February 24, 2006. Available online. http://www.imra.org/il/story.php3?id=28601.

"Bolton Admits Lebanon Truce Block." BBC News. March 27, 2007. Available online. http://news.bbc.co.uk/2/hi/middle_east/6479377.stm.

"Curriculum Vitae." Prime Minister's Office, Israel. Available online. http://www.pmo.gov.il/PMOEng/PM/Resume/.

Elon, Amos. *The Israelis: Founders and Sons.* New York: Bantam, 1972.

Erlanger, Steven. "Long on Outskirts of Power, Olmert Looks to Lead Israel." *New York Times.* March 27, 2006. Available online. http://www.nytimes.com/2006/03/27/international/middleeast/27olmert.html?_r=1&scp=1&sq=Long+on+Out

skirts+of+Power%2C+Olmert+Looks+to+Lead+Israel&st=
nyt&oref=slogin.

Fangchao, Li. "Israel Deputy PM Visits Grandpa's Harbin Grave." *China Daily.* Available online. http://www. chinadaily.net/english/doc/2004-06-26/content_342861.htm.

Farrell, Stephen. "The Times Interview with Ehud Olmert: Full Transcript." *Times* (London) Online. August 2, 2006. Available online. http://www.timesonline.co.uk/tol/news/ world/middle_east/article698343.ece.

Flesh, Ehud. "Biography: Ehud Olmert." *Jerusalem Post.* Available online. http://www.jpost.com/servlet/Satellite?cid= 1139395376017&pagename=JPost/JPArticle/ShowFull.

Halevi, Yossi Klein. "Unwanted Man." *New Republic.* October 10, 2006. Available online. http://www.tnr.com/doc.mhtml?i =20061016&s=halevi101606.

"Israel's Prime Minister, Ehud Olmert." Ynetnews.com. Available online. http://www.ynetnews.com/articles/ 0,7340,L-3283691,00.html.

Keenan, Brian. "After the Flood." *Guardian.* July 22, 2006. Available online. http://www.guardian.co.uk/syria/ story/0,,1826371,00.html.

Labott, Elise. "Israel Authorizes 'Severe' Response to Abductions." CNN. July 12, 2006. Available online. http:// www.cnn.com/2006/WORLD/meast/07/12/mideast.

Laquer, Walter, and Barry Rubin, eds. *The Israel-Arab Reader: A Documentary History of the Middle East Conflict.* New York: Penguin Books, 1984.

Levey, Gregory. "Israel's Olmert Rises from the Rubble." Salon. com. July 3, 2007. Available online. http://www.salon.com/ opinion/feature/2007/07/03/olmert/print.html.

Leyden, Joel. "Israel Exit Polls: Ehud Olmert Next Prime Minister." Israel News Agency. March 28, 2007. Available online. http://www.israelnewsagency.com/olmertisraelelectionssharon480328.html.

"Nasrallah Wins the War." *Economist.* August 19, 2006. Available online. http://www.highbeam.cm/DocPrint.aspx?DocID=1G1:149610529.

Olmert, Ehud. "Address by Acting PM Ehud Olmert to the 6th Herzliya Conference." Embassy of Israel. January 24, 2006. Available online. http://www.israelemb.org/articles/2006/January/2006012601.htm.

Olmert, Ehud. "Address by Prime Minister to Joint Meeting of U.S. Congress." Embassy of Israel. May 24, 2006. Available online. http://www.israelemb.org/articles/2006/May/2006052400.htm.

Olmert, Linda. "Mordechai Olmert." Museum of the Jewish People. Available online. http://www.bh.org.il/Communities/Archive/Harbin.asp.

"Olmert: We Were Attacked by a Sovereign Country." Ynetnews.com. Available online. http://www.ynetnews.com/articles/0,7340,L-3274385,00.html.

"Olmert's Dovish Family." *Israel Today.* May 18, 2006. Available online. http://www.israeltoday.co.il/default.aspx?tabid=128&view=item&idx=1013.

"Profile: Ehud Olmert." BBC News. Available online. http://news.bbc.co.uk/2/hi/middle_east/4134680.stm.

"Profile: Olmert Now Centre Stage." BBC News. Available online. http://news.bbc.co.uk/2.hi/middle_east/4596172.stm.

Remnick, David. "The Seventh Day: Why the Six-Day Is Still Being Fought." *New Yorker.* May 28, 2007. Available online.

http://www.newyorker.com/artists/critics/books/2007/05/28/
070528crbo_books_remnick.

Rosenberg, M.J. "Olmert's Bombshell." Israel Policy Forum.
Volume 1.72. December 10, 2003. Available online. http://
www.ipforum.org/display.cfm?rid=926.

Shabi, Rachel. "The Unlikely First Lady." *Guardian.* May 5,
2006. Available online. http://www.guardian.co.uk/israel/
Story/0,,1768101,00.html.

Taub, Gadi. "Ehud Olmert's Vision for Israel: Virtually Normal."
New Republic. May 23, 2006. Available online. http://www.tnr.
com/doc.mhtml?i=20060529&s=taub052906.

Urquhart, Conal, and Chris McGreal. "Israelis Invade Lebanon
After Soldiers Are Seized." *Guardian.* July 12, 2006. Available
online. http://www.guardian.co.uk/world/2006/jul/12/
israelandthepalestinians.lebanon.

Verter, Yossi, Mazal Mualem, and Nir Hasson. "The Winograd
Report: Lebanon War Probe Accuses Olmert of 'Serious
Failures,' Blasts Halutz, Peretz." Haaretz.com. April 30, 2007.
Available online. http://haaretz.com/hasen/spages/853705.
html.

Whitfield, Fredricka. "Interview with Jerusalem Mayor Ehud
Olmert." CNN. March 9, 2002. Available online. http://
edition.cnn.com/TRANSCRIPTS/0203/09/bn.04.html.

Wilson, Scott. "Pullout Focuses Israel on Its Future."
Washington Post. August 13, 2005. Available online.
http://www.washingtonpost.com/wp-dyn/content/
article/2005/08/12/AR2005081201546.html.

Wolff, Sarah. "Ehud Olmert: Likud, Legacy and Leadership."
American Chronicle. March 9, 2006. Available online.

http://www.americanchronicle.com/articles/view/Article.
asp?articleID=6698.

Zahn, Paula. "Interview with Ehud Olmert, Mayor of
Jerusalem." CNN. March 29, 2002. Available online. http://
transcripts.cnn.com/TRANSCRIPTS/0203/29/bn.08.html.

FURTHER READING

Barakat, Ibtsiam. *Tasting the Sky: A Palestinian Childhood.* New York: Farrar, Straus and Giroux, 2007.

Ellis, Deborah. *Three Wishes: Palestinian and Israeli Children Speak.* Toronto: Groundwood Books, 2006.

Finkelstein, Norman H. *Ariel Sharon.* Minneapolis: Lerner Publishing Group, 2005.

Frank, Mitch. *Understanding the Holy Land: Answering Questions About the Israeli-Palestinian Conflict.* New York: Viking Juvenile, 2005.

Greenfield, Howard. *A Promise Fulfilled: Theodor Herzl, Chaim Weizmann, David Ben-Gurion, and the Creation of the State of Israel.* New York: HarperTeen, 2005.

Kass, Pnina Moed. *Real Time.* Boston: Clarion Books, 2004.

Katz, Samuel M. *Jerusalem or Death: Palestinian Terrorism.* Minneapolis: Lerner Publishing Group, 2003.

Laird, Elizabeth, and Sonia Nimr. *A Little Piece of Ground.* Chicago: Haymarket Books, 2006.

Potok, Chaim. *Wanderings: History of the Jews.* New York: Fawcett, 1987.

Schroeter, Daniel J. *Israel: An Illustrated History.* New York: Oxford University Press, 1999.

Woodward, John. *Israel* (Opposing Viewpoints). Farmington Hills, MI: Greenhaven Press, 2005.

WEB SITES

Embassy of Israel Kids' Web Site
http://www.israelemb.org/kids/

Information about the history of Israel, facts, symbols, and general information.

The Jewish Children's Learning Network
http://www.akhlah.com/israel/israel.php

Israeli history, geography, and biographies, and information on holidays and traditions.

PHOTO CREDITS

126

INDEX

128

About the Authors

DENNIS ABRAMS attended Antioch College, where he majored in English and communications. A voracious reader since the age of three, Dennis is a freelance writer who has written numerous books for young adult readers, including biographies of Hamid Karzai, Ty Cobb, Eminem, Anthony Horowitz, and Xerxes. He lives in Houston, Texas, with his partner of nineteen years.

ARTHUR SCHLESINGER, JR. is remembered as the leading American historian of our time. He won the Pulitzer Prize for his books *The Age of Jackson* (1945) and *A Thousand Days* (1965), which also won the National Book Award. Schlesinger was the Albert Schweitzer Professor of the Humanities at the City University of New York and was involved in several other Chelsea House projects, including the series *Revolutionary War Leaders*, *Colonial Leaders*, and *Your Government*.